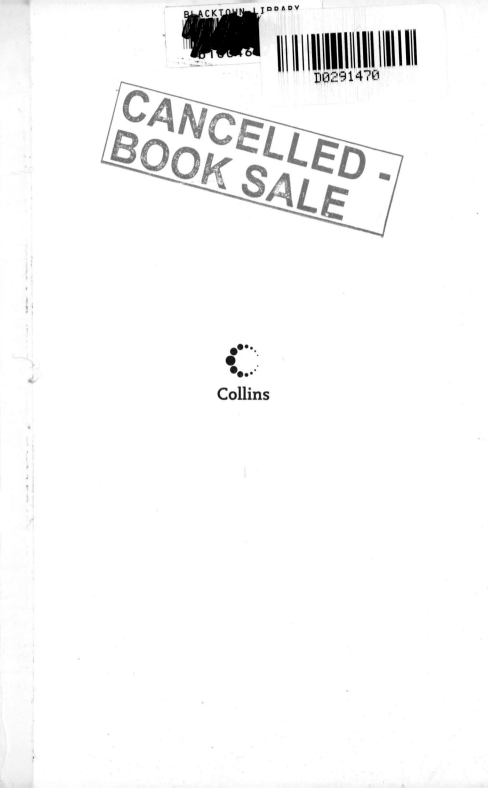

Collins

need to know?

Codes and Ciphers

Sean Callery

Collins

First published in 2006 by Collins
an imprint of
HarperCollins Publishers
77–85 Fulham Palace Road
London W6 8JB

www.collins.co.uk

Collins is a registered trademark of
HarperCollins Publishers Ltd

A catalogue record for this book is available from
the British Library

Produced by Lyra Publications
Managing editor: Emma Callery
Designer: Bob Vickers
Illustrations: Anthony Duke

For Collins
Series design: Mark Thomson

ISBN-10: 0-00-722803-1
ISBN-13: 978-0-00-722803-4

Printed and bound by Printing Express Ltd, Hong Kong

Contents

Introduction

Alice is driving to work. She hardly registers the *road signs* that guide her journey to the station. There she selects a newspaper and a book of *su doku* puzzles, pausing while the *bar codes* are scanned before she hands over her credit card. She keys in her *PIN* and pauses while the scanner *securely completes the transaction.* On the train she sits next to Bob, whose laptop whirrs into action after he types in his *password.* She decides to have a go at the *crossword* in her paper ...

A world shaped by codes

We could follow Alice and Bob through their day, continuing, as you will have noticed, to highlight in *italics* every occasion on which codes enter their lives. Codes are part of our world and of our history, too. Indeed, they have helped to shape it: Greek generals in ancient times used them to give secret orders; Wellington's defeat of Napoleon in the Peninsular Wars was partly due to his staff's ability to read coded messages sent by the French army; and, of course, many people are now aware that the course of World War II was changed by the achievements of Allied cryptographers in breaking German and Japanese ciphers.

Since the emergence of writing, people have at times felt a need to conceal or mystify the meaning of some of their communications, trying to keep control of who gains access to the knowledge it holds. One of the earliest examples is a recipe for pottery glaze that was considered too valuable to be left for just anyone to read.

The story of code making is also the story of code breaking. This book begins with a chapter looking at ancient writing such as Egyptian hieroglyphics, which, over time, became a code, as the knowledge of how to read them was washed away with the sands. This section also deals with other codes used in the past – from the hobo code used by tramps to brief feloow wanders on dangers and opportunities in the vicinity, to the phone texting codes so beloved of many teenagers today.

The book also studies codes devised not to conceal but to allow efficient, fast and often cheaper communication: Morse code, flag-signalling systems and sign language, all of which are baffling until you are let in on the secret.

From there, we take a tour through the world of codes and ciphers (learning the differences between them on the way) starting with fairly simple methods, such as the Caesar shift used in Roman times. Where relevant, each code is put into historical context (although this is not a history book, there is a 'code chronology' showing key events in the story of codes and code breaking).

Creating messages

The book explains how to create messages using such codes, and how they can be broken. People tend to assume that a code they have created will be very hard to break, when, in fact, most basic codes can be cracked in a very short time. *Codes and Ciphers* studies just how this is done, including the use of cryptanalysts' tools, such as frequency analysis – using knowledge about how common some letters are in comparison to others (see pages

82–5). A code-breaking checklist is also provided on pages 177–81.

The vast majority of codes described in this book can be re-created (and broken) using no more than pencil, paper and perseverance. Undertaking such tasks will take you back in time to the code-breaking black chambers. As explorers and conquerors travelled greater distances in search of power and wealth, their need for secret communication increased, and messengers would walk and ride with encrypted communications hidden in their clothing, bodies or equipment.

Naturally, this fostered a mini-industry of code breakers working in secret to break the code of any intercepted messages. The rooms these hidden officials occupied became known as the black chambers (see pages 152–5). They still exist; they've just got a lot bigger (see the references to GCHQ and the NSA on page 154). In an age in which communications are bounced around the globe via satellites, interception has never been easier, and governments continue to try to keep sensitive communication secret, and to peep into the inbox of other states and groups, such as terrorists, when the opportunity arises.

Looking to the future

The age of pencil and paper has passed, for since the middle of the 20th century, machines have been employed increasingly to create and to break codes. The demands of code breakers have directly led to the development of the modern computer. The tools of today's cryptographers read like a code themselves: symmetric encryption, message authentication codes, public key encryption, one-way hash functions, digital signature schemes and random number generators. Their uses are legion, from allowing you to buy things on the internet knowing that no one will (or should) be able to steal your financial details and your money, to protecting us from a maniac maverick pushing a button and launching a nuclear missile.

Cryptography has become a big business. There is heated debate about the most secure methods of sending sensitive diplomatic, scientific and business information, and a growing controversy about whether and when governments have the right to read private communications. The subject has entered the curriculum of universities and colleges, and data security is an industry in itself. The subject continues to fascinate, for its history, the intellectual challenge of creating and breaking codes, and as a leisure activity in puzzles, such as word searches, crosswords and the craze for su doku number conundrums.

Code conventions

Throughout this book, as in the convention for code writing, the term 'plaintext' refers to the original message, which is altered by encoding or encipherment. Plaintext is written in upper and lower case writing; all codes and ciphers appear in capitals.

Another convention is the names of Alice and Bob used in this introduction because it has become a convention in the field of cryptography to use these monikers. This communicative couple only exist in the world of codes and ciphers. There is more on this (and their foe Eve) on page 140.

must know

Spot the code
The ciphertexts opposite each chapter opener use the heading itself as their plaintext. On page 10, the text is spelt out using the optical telegraph alphabet from page 27. 'Secret communication' on page 38 is written in Pig Latin – see page 44. Page 54 has text substituted using the pigpen cipher on page 78. The encryption on page 86 uses the alternating cipher alphabet method shown on page 94. 'Code wars' on page 110 is fractionated and then enciphered using the keyword 'zebra' as on page 114 – the presence of four nulls being indicated by the final letter D (fourth in the alphabet). The page 132 text is written in ASCII code (see page 136). Finally, 'Codes and culture' (page 158) is enciphered using a method from one of the 'Shadow' stories (see page 160).

1 Open communication

Not all codes are secret. Some are designed to allow rapid communication in different circumstances, such as disability or distance. This chapter deals with codes where the aim is the opposite of concealment. However, it begins with the stories of two codes whose meanings were lost with time, and which became some of the oldest mysteries in the world.

Codes from the past

Anything that we cannot read is, in effect, a code that we need to break. If it is a language, we can learn it or find someone to translate the message. But what if the very language has disappeared?

From the sands of time

The story that Egyptian hieroglyphics tell is of a highly organized and capable civilization that collapsed and was forgotten for thousands of years. Much of what we now know about it has been learned from reading its writings on walls and papyrus, and the process of discovering how to read these is similar to the code-breaking methods that helped to shorten World War II. So, in a sense, hieroglyphics became the earliest codes, even though their meaning was not originally disguised. The structures on which hieroglyphics were carved or drawn collapsed, or were buried by the desert sand, while others were defaced by Christians intent on destroying remnants of a pagan past.

Hieroglyphics are pictorial writing: brightly coloured images both simple and complex. Various attempts were made to read them, but it took many years for people to realize that the pictures stood for sounds (as we might draw a bee to represent the sound 'b') of a language that had since died.

The key to unlocking this ancient mystery was the translation of the Rosetta stone. This was a man-sized black granite rock, inscribed in three different languages, unearthed by French soldiers knocking down a wall in the town of Rosetta in 1799.

---

must know

Hieroglyphs

▶ The word 'hieroglyphs' comes from the Greek language and means 'sacred carvings'.

▶ They were cut into the stone of significant buildings, such as temples and tombs, or painted onto the interior walls.

▶ The earliest date back at least 3,000 years.

Egyptian hieroglyphics were intricate and colourful and were used to tell stories and demonstrate the power of the pharoahs to their subjects.

The three-quarter-tonne stone was (reluctantly, after an attempt to sneak it away on a boat) handed over to occupying British forces and taken to the British Museum in London, where it still stands.

Its value was that the three scripts carried the same message in a trio of languages: Greek, hieroglyphics and demotic (which is a later Egyptian language derived from hieroglyphics). Historians were able to translate the Greek text and establish that it announced a decree issued by King Ptolemy V in 196 BC. It begins: 'The new king, having received the kingship from his father ...'. For a code breaker, knowing the meaning of the message you wish to unravel is gold dust.

The stone featured 1,410 hieroglyphs compared with 486 Greek words, which suggested that individual hieroglyphs did not necessarily represent whole words, and must therefore represent sounds. After some valuable groundbreaking work by Thomas Young, the stone was finally translated by Frenchman Jean François Champollion in 1823. Knowing that royal names were contained in oval shapes known as cartouches, he made the key discovery that Ptolemy's name was written bit by bit as p-t-o-l-m-y-s, proving it by finding the same symbols used for the shared sounds 'p', 't', 'o' and 'l' in writings about the famous queen Cleopatra.

This wonderful discovery was the key that opened the door of understanding the language of hieroglyphics and allowed archaeologists to learn to read other ancient Egyptian writings, shedding fresh light on the world of pharaohs, such as Rameses, and the many gods, such as the sun god Ra.

Secrets from the labyrinth

The story of how seemingly incomprehensible tablets dating back some 3,000 years finally revealed their secrets has a bizarre twist, showing that in code breaking there is no substitute for diligent, logical work, even if it reveals the opposite of what you expect.

Into the Odyssey

In 1900, archaeologist Sir Arthur Evans dug up a huge quantity of clay tablets on the island of Crete. They dated from up to 1800 BC, and had survived because they were baked in a fire that had destroyed the buildings around them in the old city of Knossos. Evans became convinced that the indecipherable writing on them was an ancient language, which he dubbed Minoan after King Minos, whose palace he had discovered. The palace is the setting for Homer's story of Theseus and the Minotaur, where our hero defeats a vicious beast that lived in a labyrinth of tunnels under the palace. Homer's tales in *The Odessy* had been dismissed as fanciful legends until the discovery of the original city of Troy in 1872.

On the tablets there were two kinds of writings, Linear A and Linear B (see box, right), and Evans spent many years trying to unscramble them. In sometimes bitter squabblings with other academics, he was particularly vicious in his treatment of those who suggested the tablets could be written in some form of ancient Greek. He never found out that he was utterly wrong. The truth was pieced together with infinite patience over a number of years by a trio of academics.

Changed endings

First, American Alice Kober noticed that some of the words in the younger text, known as Linear B, appeared in three forms, with their endings changed – just as verb endings in the English language vary to show the subject (I, you, he, she, we or they) or tense (past or present), and as nouns change when they are plural. She also found relationships between some of the 90 distinct characters, identifying some as consonants and others as vowels.

must know

The writing on the tablets
Two distinct kinds of writing were identified:
▶ Linear A (dating from 1800 BC), and
▶ Linear B, younger by 350 years.
▶ No one has ever been able to read Linear A. It is thought to be the language of Minoa prior to its conquest by the Myceneans in c.1420 BC.

Her work was continued by Michael Ventris, who studied where in a word certain characters could be found and was able to pick out single vowels, as opposed to the syllables, which were, so far, the limit of understanding. From this he deciphered signs to represent place names such as Knossos and Amnisos (another town still in existence in modern Crete). Because the tablets were known to be inventories, with lists of easily identified numbers (the material seems to have been a sort of *Domesday Book*), he identified by its position the word for 'total', and found it was very similar to archaic Greek.

Ventris linked up with a cryptanalyst with a good knowledge of ancient Greek and in 1953 they were able to prove that Linear B was indeed written in the Greek of 3,000 years before. Their findings contradicted the beliefs of the man who found the tablets, Sir Arthur Evans (who had died in 1940), and of most other analysts.

The saga reveals the value of diligent, logical, unbiased research by people who are able to keep their minds open to all possibilities in trying to break a code.

More past secrets

Among the early forms of written communication is cuneiform writing, in which letters are carved onto tablets (cuneiform means 'wedge writing'). As their meanings were lost in time, these writings became codes concealing secrets of the past. Early writing used different characters for syllables, but later languages, such as the Ugaritic script (which dates back to the 14th century BC), were based on an alphabet. There is plenty of evidence that meanings were concealed even in early writings, and the practice continued through the centuries.

▶ There are records of secret writing that were being used for political communication in India in the 4th century BC, and the erotic textbook, the *Kama Sutra*, lists it as one of the skills women should learn.

▶ Early antecedents of the Kurds in northern Iraq employed cryptic script in holy books to keep their religion secret from their Muslim neighbours.

▶ A mixed-up alphabet carved onto a wooden tablet and thought to date from 7th-century Egypt is believed to be the world's oldest cipher key.

▶ Medieval monastic scribes entertained themselves by adding messages in simple ciphers to the margins of texts they were copying out.

▶ An extraordinary 12th-century nun called Hildegard of Bingen constructed an alternative alphabet and created a new cryptic language, called Lingua Ignota, claiming the inspiration for it came through visions.

▶ Franciscan Friar Roger Bacon wrote about cryptography in his *Secret Works of Art and the Nullity of Magic* in the 13th century, listing seven different kinds of secret writing.

▶ Medieval builders carved masonic symbols into the stone of structures they were working on, partly as a sort of signature and possibly to help decide how much each should be paid.

▶ The alchemists of the Middle Ages concealed their identities and formulae with code marks.

Heraldry

Heraldry is an early example of a code being used for easy identification. Medieval knights would wear certain colours and symbols, which came to be known as their 'coat of arms'. Some believe this was for rapid identification of the knight and their followers on the battlefield, others that it was inspired by vanity and the desire to show social status. Either way, by 1400 you had to have a coat of arms if you wanted to participate in a tournament. Families could select their own design, combining it with that of any families they married into. A language of heraldry developed, for example, gold suggested generosity and green indicated hope, while each design element and symbol carried its own meaning. For more information, see www.theheraldrysociety.com and www.college-of-arms.gov.uk.

A trio of historic American codes

Native American tribes used smoke signals to send simple messages over long distances, working to a pre-arranged code. The practice was common in ancient China, and is still carried out by boy scouts today.

Many such puffs of smoke were most likely signalling the activities of the cowboys raising cattle on the land. To prove ownership of their beasts, these men also had their own branding alphabet based on three elements: letters or numbers, geometric shapes, and pictorial symbols. Originating in the 18th century, they were designed to quickly identify cows over long distances and partly to combat cattle rustling (see box, left).

good to know

Old brands

Cattle branding has been traced back 6,000 years to the Ancient Egyptians – tomb paintings show it taking place. There is also biblical evidence that Jacob branded his livestock.

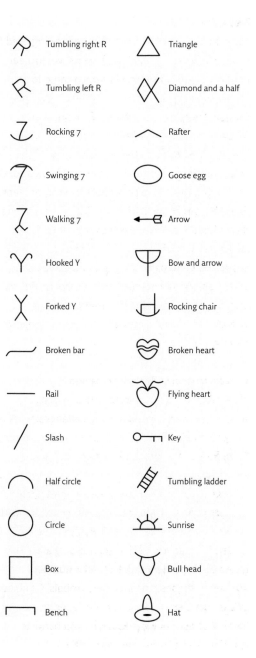

Tumbling right R	Triangle
Tumbling left R	Diamond and a half
Rocking 7	Rafter
Swinging 7	Goose egg
Walking 7	Arrow
Hooked Y	Bow and arrow
Forked Y	Rocking chair
Broken bar	Broken heart
Rail	Flying heart
Slash	Key
Half circle	Tumbling ladder
Circle	Sunrise
Box	Bull head
Bench	Hat

Some examples of the cowboy branding alphabet.

	Halt		Officer
	Danger		Gentleman
	Nothing to gain		You can camp here
	Unsafe place		Be prepared to defend yourself
	Road spoilt		Owner is in
	Safe camp		Owner is out
	If sick, will care for you		Doctor
	Dishonest man		Kind-hearted woman
	Man with a gun		Vicious dog
	Be quiet		Woman
	Afraid		Go! March on!

Some examples of the hobo symbols.

Hobos, who travelled around the US in the 19th century, developed a code of marks chalked outside houses to inform fellow tramps what kind of reception they could expect. The signs had meanings such as:

▶ Doctor
▶ Danger
▶ Safe camp
▶ If sick, will care for you
▶ You can sleep in the hayloft.
(See the illustrations, left.)

Cars, books and groceries

There are many codes playing a role in modern life:

▶ The International Standard Book Number (ISBN) has been used to identify books since 1970. The 10- or 13-digit code holds information on the country of origin or language, publisher and item number.

▶ Barcodes make information readable by a scanner. Early versions stored data in widths and gaps between parallel lines, but today they also come in patterns of dots, concentric circles and hidden in images.

▶ Number plates allow identification of motor vehicles, which also often have coded numbers identifying the chassis and engine.

▶ Pin codes are personal identification numbers used to authenticate identities, frequently in financial transactions.

▶ A postcode (or zip code in the US) is a series of letters and/or digits identifying a location, used for sorting mail and storing geographical data.

Visual systems

Numerous codes have been devised to aid communication, reflecting changes in the world over the last few hundred years: these signal codes enable the passing on of information over long distances.

Duty free
The navy had already agreed numerous short cuts in their flag code so that complete words did not need to be spelt out. Thus, in the famous signal sent by Lord Nelson before the Battle of Trafalgar in 1805, 'England expects that every man will do his D-U-T-Y', only the final word was spelt in full.

Semaphore

Semaphore is the common term for a system of signalling using a pair of flags, devised in 1817 by Captain Marryat of the British Royal Navy, who adapted it from the organization's flag code of 1799. Although clearly developed for use at sea, the Marryat Code, or the Universal Code of Signals, as it is also known, is just as effective on land.

The flags are usually divided diagonally into red and yellow, and are moved like independent hands on a clock face. Each position represents a letter, so messages are spelt out. There are also set signals for recurring content, such as 'Error' and 'End', while the digits zero to nine are represented by the first eleven letters of the alphabet (J also doubles up as 'Letters follow') when preceded by the message 'Numbers follow'.

It is said that the semaphore flag system was the fastest method of visual communication at sea – quicker than a flashing light using Morse code (see page 32) – and was valuable in the modern era as it allowed ships to send each other messages while maintaining radio silence. (See also International signal flags, pages 24–5.)

The semaphore code allows for clear communication across long distances without breaking radio silence.

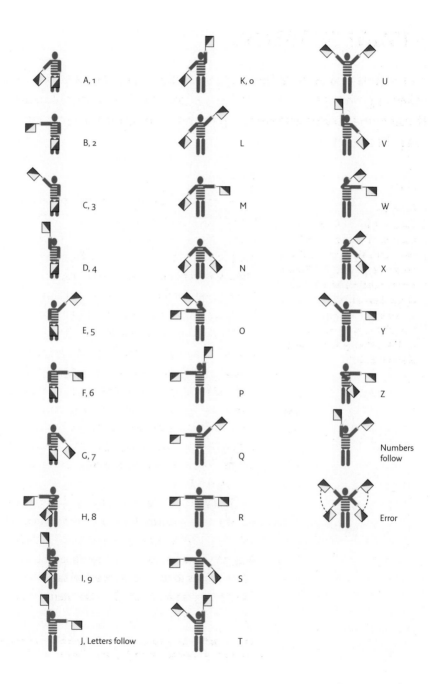

International signal flags

This is a system of flags, one for each letter of the alphabet, which can be used to communicate at sea. Ships commonly display the flags to give their four- or five-letter radio call sign. In addition to representing a letter or number, each of the 40 flags carries a message for common situations at sea:

International signal flags play a crucial role in enabling communication between people who do not share a common language.

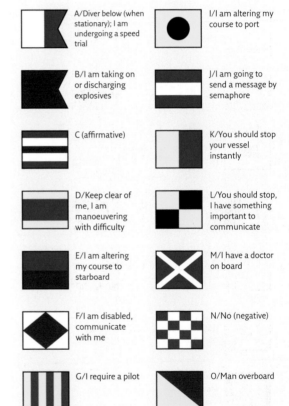

A/Diver below (when stationary); I am undergoing a speed trial

I/I am altering my course to port

B/I am taking on or discharging explosives

J/I am going to send a message by semaphore

C (affirmative)

K/You should stop your vessel instantly

D/Keep clear of me, I am manoeuvering with difficulty

L/You should stop, I have something important to communicate

E/I am altering my course to starboard

M/I have a doctor on board

F/I am disabled, communicate with me

N/No (negative)

G/I require a pilot

O/Man overboard

H/I have a pilot on board

P/The Blue Peter – all aboard, vessel is about to proceed to sea. (At sea) your lights are out or burning badly

two-letter signals for emergencies, three letters for general information. This is particularly useful when ships are trying to communicate without a common language.

 Q/My vessel is healthy and I request free practique

 R/The way is off my ship. You may feel your way past me.

 S/My engines are going full speed astern

 T/Do not pass ahead of me

 U/You are standing into danger

 V/I require assistance (not distress)

 W/I require medical assistance

X/Stop carrying out your intentions and watch for my signals

Y/I am carrying mails

Z/To be used to address or call shore stations

Distress

Answering pennant

Numeric pennants

0

1

2

3

4

5

6

7

8

9

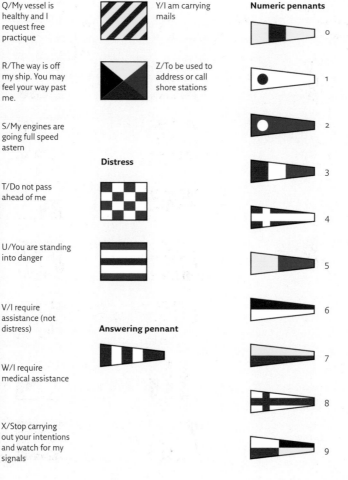

The optical telegraph

Copper pans, a clock face, a set of pulleys and the telescope all made a contribution to the development of a coded communication system that had a major impact on 19th-century Europe, but is now almost forgotten.

We tend to assume that telegrams were the first system allowing rapid communication over long distances. In fact, it had to fight to take over from one that was already in place. Developed by French brothers Claude and René Chappe, its first incarnation in 1790 used two synchronized clocks with speeded-up second hands and a code system for each number on the clock face. Each brother took his place by one of the clocks, positioned several hundred metres apart. When Claude banged his casserole, René noted down the number shown on his clock. In this way they were able to communicate simple messages.

Speed of light

Light travels faster and more efficiently than sound, and they soon replaced the casserole with a single reversible black-and-white panel, still sending messages using the position of the hand on the clock face. The optical telegraph was born. When they demonstrated this in 1791, the range was ten miles – revolutionary at a time when the fastest messages travelled at the speed of a galloping horse.

The signalling system evolved into using five sliding black-and-white panels, which offered 32 coding combinations. Two years on, Claude Chappe decided this was too complicated and, probably influenced by the navy's use of flags, switched to a

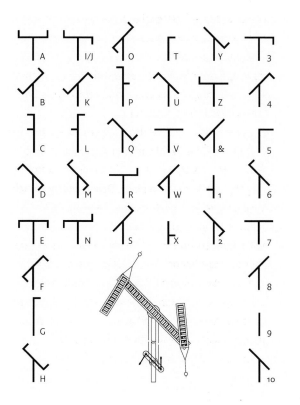

The optical telegraph revolutionized communication by allowing messages to be sent long distance at previously unheard of speeds.

movable beam with angled arms that mimicked a person holding a pair of flags in different positions (see the illustration, above).

Hours into minutes

On 16 July 1794, the first official line, using 22 stations to link Paris and Lille, was brought into service, sending messages 150 miles in a matter of minutes when a courier on horseback would have taken 30 hours. Within a few years, a 3,125-mile network of more than 500 signalling stations was set up across French territory. They were placed on hills, castle towers and rooftops. Hauling on ropes and pulleys, the operators

Telegraph reader
In the 1850 novel *David Copperfield*, Charles Dickens describes Mr Dick as, 'making a veritable telegraph of himself by his gesticulations to Miss Betsy Trotwood', showing that his readers would have known what an optical telegraph looked like in action.

now had 196 signalling 'pictures', and the system was christened the semaphore telegraph. Its principal value was military information for Napoleon, but other uses included the transmission of the week's winning national lottery numbers.

Other countries followed suit. For example, the British admiralty set up their own telegraph using six wooden shutters mounted on a tower to allow communication between London and the south coast because they were at war with, ironically, France.

By the mid 1830s, the spinning shutters and swivelling of telegraph towers formed lines across much of western Europe. It was expensive to run as each tower was manned by skilled operators and, of course, messages could only be sent in daylight when fog did not interfere with vision. Nevertheless, the coding system allowed for transmission of information at speeds unheard of previously. The optical telegraph reluctantly went into decline with the invention of the electric telegraph system. Claude Chappe, embroiled in arguments about ownership of the ideas behind his invention, committed suicide in 1805.

Sign language

Sign language uses the oldest coding method of all: hand signals. Although used informally since the birth of mankind, the first books describing sign language appeared in the 17th century, aiming to communicate with the deaf by using hand gestures as an exaggerated 'mouth'. There are hundreds of sign languages in use around the world, the two most common being American Sign Language (ASL, see illustration, right) and Signed English. In addition, many sports officials use standardized hand signals for some communication.

A

H

O

V

B

I

P

W

C

J

Q

X

D

K

R

Y

E

L

S

Z

F

M

T

G

N

U

Unlike Signed English (which has gestures for words), American Sign Language uses an alphabet, allowing messages to be spelt out.

The feeling code: Braille

Braille is a non-secret code that allows the blind to read. Like many codes, its origins lie in the need for the military to communicate without being detected or understood.

The young Louis Braille simplified a system of raised dots to create Braille characters (opposite).

Dark secret

The story begins with Artillery Captain Charles Barbier of Napoleon's French army in the early 1800s. Frustrated by the difficulty in reading messages safely on the front line (where smoke and the chaos of battle hindered communication, and lighting a lamp created an easy target for the enemy), he devised a code using 12 raised dots on paper, called night writing. Unfortunately, his fellow soldiers found it too difficult to learn and it was not adopted.

Thinking that it might have a role in helping the blind to read, Barbier started to visit schools for the blind. In 1821 he demonstrated his code to a group of children at the Royal Institution for Blind Youth in Paris. The audience included the 12-year-old Louis Braille, who had been blinded by accident nine years previously. Braille quickly mastered the system but found he could simplify it to use just six dots. Although he published the first Braille book in 1837, it did not catch on around the world for another 30 years.

Braille has since been adapted to nearly every language on earth and remains the major medium of literacy for blind people everywhere.

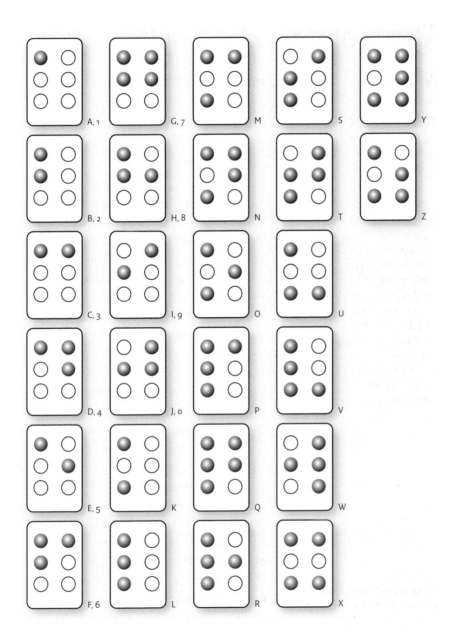

The world's most famous code: Morse

Morse code is the most famous code in the world. It allows rapid communication over long distances along wires or radio waves, or via sound or light in an easy-to-learn system of dots and dashes.

must know

Beyond the telegraph
In addition to its use in the telegraph system, Morse code was also used in these ways:
▶ When armies and navies use a heliograph (which reflects the sun's rays).
▶ Messages sent with the Aldis lamp (a powerful light used at sea).
▶ Radio messages.
▶ Airline pilots still have to know it, even today.

Code on tap

The American Samuel Morse had attempted various inventions and money-making schemes before he chanced across the opportunity of sending messages along wires. He enlisted the help of experts in the field of sending an electric pulse over long distances and in 1838 designed a code that could be tapped out by hand. Showing admirable understanding of the practicalities of communicating language, he ensured that the most frequently used letters could be entered with the least effort, thus the code for 'e' is a dot, and for 't' it is a dash.

This combination slowly won over a sceptical public and the first telegraph line, following the 40-mile railway track between Baltimore and Washington, launched in 1844 with the message: 'What hath God wrought'.

Morse code was originally treated as a novelty (public chess matches were played on it) and struggled to overtake the already established optical telegraph (see pages 26–8), but gradually its

A	·—	N	—·	0	—————
B	—···	O	———	1	·————
C	—·—·	P	·——·	2	··———
D	—··	Q	——·—	3	···——
E	·	R	·—·	4	····—
F	··—·	S	···	5	·····
G	——·	T	—	6	—····
H	····	U	··—	7	——···
I	··	V	···—	8	———··
J	·———	W	·——	9	————·
K	—·—	X	—··—		
L	·—··	Y	—·——		
M	——	Z	——··		

Morse code is designed so that the most frequently used letters require the least effort.

SOS

The dit-dit-dit-dah-dah-dah-dit-dit-dit SOS distress call does not stand for 'Save Our Souls', as many people believe. It is a code indicating that the operator will no longer be able to send messages. The lack of gaps shows that it does not represent individual letters.

advantages of cheap and very fast communication were recognized. In England, it enabled the arrest of the murderer John Tawell on 3 January 1845 when his description was sent ahead of the train on which he had fled, leading to his arrest at Paddington Station.

The telegraph system grew rapidly. Skilled operators soon learned to ignore the paper printouts of messages and instead listened to the clicking of the receiving apparatus to understand the message. They began using abbreviations for long common words or phrases and many variations of code words were introduced. This was encouraged by the thrifty public keen to keep the length of messages to a minimum as payment was by the word. In the American Civil War (1861–5), the telegraph was used widely for the first time in warfare, and it was imperative to encrypt important messages.

Banks, in particular, were keen to develop secure codes as it allowed them to transfer money electronically. By 1877, nearly $2.5 million was being telegraphed every year in nearly 40,000 separate transactions. Because the messages were legally binding contracts, even marriage ceremonies were known to be conducted using the equipment, with the bride and groom clicking out 'I do' while a congregation of telegraph operators down the line listened in.

Morse code underwent a few refinements as it continued to serve as a code in radio communication. It remained in use on the seas until it was replaced by a satellite-based communication system in 2000.

Shorthand

Another form of open code is shorthand, where abbreviations and symbols allow very fast writing. It was an essential tool in many businesses before the invention of recording and dictation machines. The earliest shorthand systems date from Greece in the 4th century BC.

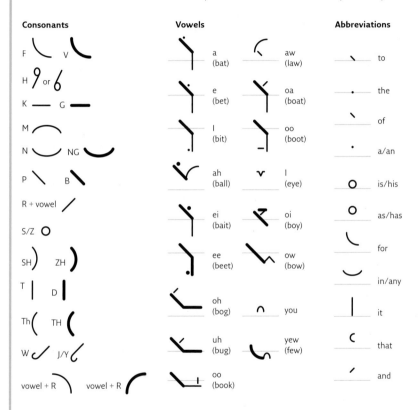

Some of the many symbols used in shorthand to represent letters and sounds. This is from a version (there are many!) of Pitman's shorthand.

New global codes

Communications technology, such as computers and mobile phones, have spawned a new set of codes aiming to save costs and time by making communication as brief as possible. These are simply modern forms of shorthand, but they also carry great social kudos for the young.

Leet

Around the world, people are creating a new code language at their keyboards, which is the digital equivalent of Pig Latin (see page 44) with a few hieroglyphics thrown in for good measure. Widely used in chat rooms, among hackers and computer gamers, leet, or leetspeak (leet is a corruption of 'elite'), enables rapid communication to take place by using keyboard characters as short cuts for sounds, words and phrases.

Some basic rules for leet are:

▶ Numbers can replace the letters they resemble, so 'leet' is '1337', 'B' (hence 'be') is represented by '8', '9' replaces 'G', '5' or '$' stands for 'S' and '4' is 'A'. Thus 'leetspeak' is '13375p34k'.

▶ Letters substitute for sounds, so words ending in C or K now end in X, and Z supplies 'S' and 'ES' endings.

However there are many variations. For example, the first three letters of the alphabet can be shown as:

A: 4,/\, @, /-\,

B: 8,6,|3, |:,P>

C: [, <, (

One of the rules of leet is that there aren't really any rules: spelling and grammar conventions are largely ignored and the idiom is constantly evolving. It is particularly popular in communication between computer gamers and hackers.

Here are a few leet words and phrases:

- k3wL = 'cool'
- m4d sk1llz = 'mad skills' – a talent
- noob = 'newbie' - a newcomer
- yo = 'yo', an alternative to 'Hi'.

Txt talk

Txt tlk, or txt lingo, is the language of the mobile phone, so it has similar aims to leet but has been adapted to suit use on a handset. However, it is also used in internet chatrooms along with leet. It developed through the introduction of the Short Messaging Service (SMS), which allows the sending of text messages of up to about 150 characters and is used for conversations and news and financial information services. The first message was sent in 1992, and just over a decade later texts were being sent at a rate of 500 billion a year.

Some basic rules for txt tlk are:

- Vowels are omitted.
- Whole words can be left out if the sense is not affected.
- SpacesAreMarkedByCapitals.

Txt words and phrases:

2 = 'to' or 'too'

4 = 'for' as in 'b4'

C = 'see'

R = 'are'

Y = 'why'

8 = the syllable 'ate' as in 'gr8' or 'm8'

bf or gf = 'boyfriend' or 'girlfriend'

thx = 'thanks'

np = 'no problem'

Keyboard or handset characters are also used to create pictorial messages such as these ones (try tilting your head if you don't see how it works):

O:-) = angel   :-! = bored   %) = confused

Ecretsay
ommunicationcay

2 Secret communication

For thousands of years, the only way to get a message to someone you couldn't talk to directly was to send it via another person. If you didn't want it read by an enemy, you had to find a way to hide it.

Hidden messages

The best place to hide a message is somewhere completely innocuous. In the course of history, messages have been concealed inside animals and people, pencils and even coins, and that humble material wax has been a friend to many a spy.

Hares and hairs

The principal motive for sending secret messages was for military or diplomatic confidentiality. Generals and senior officials wanted to know that even if their message carriers were intercepted, no one would understand what information they had with them.

The early Greek historian Herodotus, writing in about 440 BC, tells a trio of tales involving concealed messages. In the 6th century BC, Harpagus, a Median soldier, was plotting against Astyages, his own king. He wrote a message to the king's enemy, Cyrus, promising to change sides, and hid it in the belly of a hare, which was carried by a messenger in the guise of an innocent hunter. Its delivery prompted a Persian revolt against the Medians and Harpagus did indeed betray his king, who was replaced by Cyrus. The idea of hiding a message in an animal was still around in 16th-century Italy, when Giavanni Porta records the practice of feeding a message to a dog, which could then be taken on an apparently innocent trip where it would be killed to retrieve the information.

In another complicated plot, this time by the Greeks against the Persians, Histiaeus earned a place in the pantheon of secret messages. Wishing to prompt a rebellion against Darius, but stranded at court in his role as ambassador, Histiaeus had to somehow encourage his son-in-law Aristagoras to attack the city of Miletus. Clearly prepared to sacrifice speed for secrecy, Histiaeus shaved a slave's head, branded his message onto the poor man's scalp and only sent him on his way when the hair had grown over the writing. It worked: the city was taken by the Greeks and established as a democracy, prompting further rebellions against their Persian rulers.

Wax facts

In 480 BC the Persians completed a five-year military build-up and launched an attack on Athens, believing their plan to be a secret. However, a Greek called Demaratus had witnessed their preparations and managed to get a warning to his compatriots. Messages were usually sent on wax tablets, but these would obviously not be kept secret. So Demaratus instead carved his message into the wooden base of the tablet, which he then covered with wax. The blank tablets arrived without incident, but baffled their recipients until they scraped away the wax and discovered the warning. This allowed them to repel the attack, which was thought to be crucial in preserving their independence.

The Greeks were not alone in their need to communicate secretly, or in their use of wax. The ancient Chinese wrote messages onto silk, scrunched it into a little ball, which was then coated with wax. The messenger would hide or swallow the ball to conceal it during his journey. Roman historian Tacitus tells of wounded soldiers concealing writing on their bandages, of sewing messages into the soles of sandals, and even writing messages on a thin sheet of lead and rolling it into an earring. More recently, Cold War Russian spies hid microfilm in hollowed-out pencils, batteries and coins.

Invisible writing

What better way of concealing a message than rendering it invisible? It saves all the effort of devising and using a code and allows open, apparently innocent communication between people who are being observed. The technical term for this is steganography.

must know

Covert writing
▶ The term for hidden writing is steganography, from 'stega', the Greek word for roof or cover, and 'graphy', meaning writing.
▶ The practice continues today: in electrical communications it is called transmission security.

Hoodwinking inks

A number of natural materials have been used for invisible writing for thousands of years. Both the Greeks and Romans extracted such inks from nuts and plants. For example, in about AD 100 the Roman writer Pliny recorded that he could obtain a liquid from the tithymalus plant (which is part of the euphorbia family). When he wrote with it, the message vanished as the ink dried, but it reappeared when the paper was gently heated.

Pliny could have chosen one of many other organic liquids such as onion juice, vinegar and apple, and any citrus juice. All turn brown when gently heated (a hot iron, hairdryer or light bulb is best – actual fire is too hot). This knowledge has benefited secret agents across the centuries, some of whom resorted to their own urine when other supplies ran out. Cola drinks also work with this method (use the non-diet kind – sugar is required).

A large number of chemicals also function as invisible ink (also known as 'sympathetic ink'). They are activated by another chemical called the 'reagent'. Examples include iron sulphate solution, which reacts to solutions of potassium cyanate, or sodium carbonate and copper sulphate, which react to ammonia fumes.

Some of these chemicals can be harmful, so do not try this yourself unless you are a chemist or a trained spy! However, one experiment you can do is to write in milk on thick paper, using a brush rather than a pen so you don't leave any indentations on the paper. Watch as your words disappear, then rub dark powder such as ashes or charcoal across the page, and your message returns. In Nazi Germany, ballot forms were secretly numbered in milk to allow checking of how people voted in plebiscites.

Banks and amusement parks sometimes use invisible inks that shine under ultraviolet radiation known as 'blacklight'. The inks contain colour-brightening chemicals similar to those found in laundry washing powders.

Inky tricks

Sending sheets of 'blank' paper is likely to arouse suspicion, so agents writing in invisible ink do so on paper with an innocuous message, or use shopping lists or pictures as a background.

The use of invisible inks was widespread in the Middle Ages, through the Renaissance and was still an important skill for spies during World War I. German agents were by then disguising possession of such inks by impregnating items of clothing with the liquid, activating it by soaking the garment in water. In the later stages of the war, the American Military Intelligence Division MI-8 was testing 2,000 suspicious letters a week for secret ink. Its work led to the capture of German spy Maria de Victorica.

Invisible digital writing

An intriguing by-product of the internet age is the re-emergence of secret writing as a valuable tool. If you've ever been baffled by how some seemingly unrelated websites appear when you are searching for something on the net, the answer echoes the methods described above. It is possible to hide text on the screen either by typing white text on a white background, concealing it on a non-printable area of the page, or in graphics or a music file. You can't see it, but the search engines find it. This embedded text gets their website included in a wider range of search results. Some companies go a step further and hide their competitors' names on their own websites, meaning that their site pops up on the screen whenever someone keys in the name of their rival.

Steganography can also be used for secret communication, embedding data on the screen rather like a microdot hidden in a piece of punctuation. Its advantage is that an interceptor is unlikely to detect the presence of the data, allowing secure communication, albeit of fairly short messages.

Spoken codes

Speaking directly to someone else is, of course, the most efficient way of communicating, but when there is danger of other ears listening in, a spoken code is required, most of which are quite simple to break once you know the key.

Igpay Atinlay

The simplest spoken code is Pig Latin, a letter re-arrangement code that is particularly popular with children. There are three basic rules:

▶ Words that start with vowels have 'ay' added to the end, so 'actually' becomes 'actuallyay'.

▶ For words starting with a consonant, that letter is moved to the back, and then 'ay' is added at the end, so 'can' becomes 'ancay'.

▶ If two consonants are at the start, they are moved to the end, adding 'ay', so 'speak' becomes 'eakspay'.

Thus, 'Actually a child can speak Pig Latin well' is spoken as, 'Actuallyay aay ildchay ancay eakspay Igpay Atinlay ellway'. With practice, Pig Latin can be spoken and understood at quite a pace. In a variation known as Tut Latin, the sound 'tut' is added between each syllable.

Another spoken code language is Opish, in which 'op' is added after each consonant. Thus 'book' transforms into 'bopookop' and 'code' is 'copodop'. Words become very long and it becomes very hard to decipher meaning. Similar to Opish is Turkey Irish, in which 'ab' is added before every vowel sound, so 'book' becomes 'babook' and 'code' is now 'cabode'. As with Opish, this is a novelty language rather than a code that can be used for meaningful communication.

A more sophisticated spoken code disguises information. For example, just prior to the German occupation of Norway in 1940, telephone and radio calls from Nazi agents were intercepted. They appeared to be sending sales and tonnage information about fishing, but analysis showed that they were actually communicating the numbers of ships listed in the shipping bible *Lloyd's Register*.

Later in World War II, innocent-sounding calls discussing the flower market were also found to be disguised information about which ships were in harbour and the nature of repairs being undertaken.

Take a butcher's at this

Cockney rhyming slang is a spoken code that has survived for about 200 years. It substitutes (usually) two words for one, with which it rhymes. So 'butcher's' in the heading above is short for 'butcher's hook', meaning 'look'. Traditional examples are:

Apples and pears = stairs
Barnet (fair) = hair
Brown bread = dead
Canoes = shoes
Dickie Dirt = shirt
Mahatma (Ghandi) = brandy

The slang continues to develop. Here are some more recent introductions:
Basil (Fawlty) = balti
Billie (Piper) = sniper or windscreen wiper
Metal Mickey = sickie

There are various theories about how Cockney rhyming slang started. It was certainly in London's

must know

Aussie slang
Australians have their own rhyming slang, including:
After darks = sharks
Charlie (Wheeler) = sheila (woman)
Joe Blakes = snakes

did you know?

The cow in the high street
In the 1970s, a local newspaperman was in the habit of illegally listening in to police radio communication and heard a report of a cow in the high street. Unable to locate the beast, he went to the police station and asked them about it. 'You've been listening on our radio frequency,' said the sergeant.
'No I haven't,' he lied.
'Yes you have. A cow in the high street is our code for, "Your tea is ready,"' came the reply.

East End, and definitely devised to prevent other listeners from knowing what was being said. It may have originated from:

▶ Villainous builders in the London docks.
▶ Market vendors talking about customers.
▶ Prisoners who didn't want their guards to understand what they were saying.
▶ Thieves aware that Robert Peel's newly launched police force might be around.

Police code

In the UK, the police use letters to ensure accuracy in spelling out important words and phrases such as number plates. This is the police code alphabet:
Alpha, Bravo, Charlie, Delta, Echo, Foxtrot, Golf, Hotel, India, Juliet, Kilo, Lima, Mike, November, Oscar, Papa, Quebec, Romeo, Sierra, Tango, Uniform, Victor, Whisky, Yankee, Zulu.

These are just a few of the hundreds of codes and abbreviations used by police forces in the US:
10-1 You are being received poorly
10-2 You are being received clearly
10-3 Stop transmitting
10-4 OK
BOL Be on the lookout
DB Dead body
GTA Grand theft auto
J Juvenile involved
OT Over time
QT Secrecy required
Code 2 Proceed immediately with lights/without siren
Code 3 Proceed immediately with lights and siren.

Native tongues

All of the codes described so far can be broken relatively easily. One spoken code that defied analysis, however, was used by the US forces in the two world wars: a language that none of the opposing forces could understand.

In 1918, orders within Company D, 141st Infantry were openly transmitted by field telephone in complete security because they were spoken by one of eight serving Choctaws, a native American group from Oklahoma.

Other native tongues were also used. The unique advantage was that these languages had developed geographically and linguistically far away from other peoples and conveyed meanings with precise pronunciation and hesitations, which were unintelligible to outsiders.

The practice was repeated in World War II, when as many as 420 Navajo speakers were used by the marines in the Pacific combat zone, baffling Japanese intelligence personnel.

Across the airwaves

Spoken codes were also used in BBC radio broadcasts during World War II. Known as jargon codes, these were short phrases with hidden meanings that were agreed in advance. 'William waits for Mary', for example, informed one resistance group that supplies would be dropped for them at the agreed location at midnight. The signal announcing the D-Day invasion in 1944 was the broadcasting of the song 'Chanson d'Automne' by Paul Verlaine.

Words within words

Hiding words within words has proved to be a popular method of secret communication as it is very hard to detect, the carrier text being an everyday innocuous message.

Reading between the lines

In 17th- and 18th-century Britain, it was very expensive to send letters by post, but sending newspapers was cheaper, even, at times, free. Thrifty communicators seized on this and adopted the puncture code that had been described by Greek historian Aeneas the Tactician 2,000 years before.

They would make small pinpricks, or mark tiny dots, over certain letters so that they could spell out a message, which could then be cheaply dispatched to their correspondent. The practice continued until postage prices were altered in the middle of the 19th century. However, German spies used this exact system during World War I, and again in World War II, this time using invisible ink.

The disadvantage of this method is that a lot of the carrier text is redundant, so many words are delivered from which only fairly short messages can be communicated. The next logical step is to write your own 'carrier' message, which can be decoded with an agreed formula.

A simple example of this is an acrostic: a sentence in which the initial letters spell out a separate message. These are called null ciphers and are often employed in puzzles and crosswords. For example, cuddly attack tiger spells CAT. They are also used as memory aides, for example BRASS is an acronym for how to shoot a rifle: Breath, Relax, Aim, Sight, Squeeze, and the sentence Every Good Boy Deserves Favour sets out the letters on the lines of sheet music when written in the treble clef.

This method is thought to be the inspiration for the Christian sign of the fish. In the early days of this religion, when it was necessary at times to keep your faith secret, ancient Greek was widely spoken. The phrase 'Jesus Christ Son of God, Saviour' rendered in ancient Greek is 'Iesous Christos Theou Uios Soter'. The first letters spell ICHTHUS, the Greek word for 'fish'. So followers of Jesus could use a fish sign, or the word ICHTHUS, to show that they were Christian.

A coded escape

In general, devising an innocent-sounding acrostic message that makes sense is very tricky. However, choosing to send a message via, say, every third letter is far easier to devise, and harder to spot. A famous example of this is the story from the English Civil War of Sir John Trevanion, a royalist locked into Colchester Castle awaiting probable execution by his Cromwellian captors. He received this letter:

'Worthie Sir John: Hope, that is ye beste comfort of ye afflicated, cannot much, I fear me, help you now. That I would saye to you, is this only: if ever I may be able to requite that I do owe you, stand not upon asking me. Tis not much that I can do: but what I can do, bee ye verie sure I wille.

I knowe that, if dethe comes, if ordinary men fear it, it frights not you, accounting it for a high honour, to have such a rewarde of your loyalty. Pray yet that you may be spared this soe bitter, cup. I fear not that you will grudge any sufferings; only if bie submission you can turn them away, 'tis the part of a wise man. Tell me, an if you can, to do for you anythinge that you wolde have done. The general goes back on Wednesday. Restinge your servant to command, - R.T.'

On the surface this is a verbose, ineffectual statement of loyalty, and the guards charged with checking his letters could find nothing suspicious. But take out every third letter after a punctuation mark and it creates the more useful message: PANEL AT EAST END OF CHAPEL SLIDES. Sir John promptly asked to be allowed to pray at the chapel, and made his escape. Some historians question details of this tale, but it does illustrate the value of an acrostic code.

A similar strategy was used by a German spy in World War II, whose message: 'Apparently neutral's protest is thoroughly discounted and ignored. Isman hard hit. Blockade issue affects pretext for embargo on by-products, ejecting suets and vegetable oils,' spells out 'Pershing sails from NY June 1' if you only read the second letter of each word.

A similar simple encoding method is to conceal the true message with extra words, and include guidance on how to identify which words to read. For example, the 1/4 at the start of this message instructs the reader to ignore the first and every

fourth word: 'Tom: 1/4 gifts do not arrive often
father will be pleased here, Lucy' so the plaintext
reads: 'Tom do not arrive father will be here, Lucy.'

Windows 1550

Another method of sending a message concealed on
a page of writing is the stencil method, in which the
hidden text is read through 'windows' cut into card
or fabric laid over the letter.

The Cardano grille

This code was invented by an Italian doctor and
mathematician called Girolamo Cardano in 1550 and
is known as the Cardano grille. Small holes were
punched in an irregular pattern in a piece of card,
which was used as an overlay on top of a letter. This
method allows for reading only single letters at a
time, but it can be adapted to use larger holes so
that syllables or whole words appear in the window,

---

must know

Cardano (1501–76) is one of history's intriguing characters.
He was active in medicine, mathematics, astronomy,
science, chess and gambling.
▶ He published 131 books and left behind another 111 that
were unpublished.
▶ Two of his books were on cryptography.
▶ He wrote the first great book on algebra, and a book on
the use of probability to aid gambling.
▶ He suggested a form of writing for the blind based on
touch, hundreds of years ahead of Braille.
▶ This colourful character is said to have killed himself in
1576 to fulfil his own astrological prediction of the date of
his death.

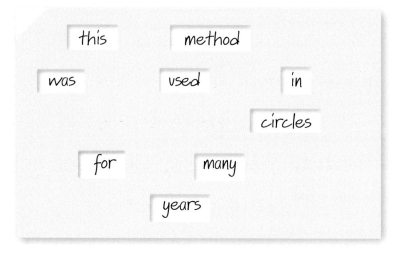

First you write your message in the windows ...

... then you remove the top card ...

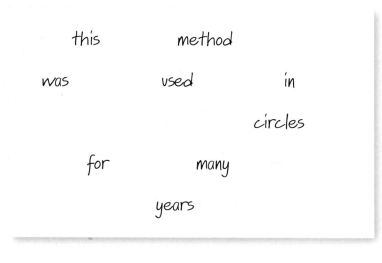

Today this is not a method anyone teaches. It was sometimes used by artists in official symbols because squares and circles are better for producing many simple designs without years of practice.

... and, finally, fill in the paper to create an innocuous message that will not arouse suspicion.

although this then makes it more difficult to disguise the message.

Provided the same card with cut-outs is not used more than a few times, the method is safe, and it was certainly widely used in diplomatic correspondence for hundrds of years after its invention. The system also requires there to be two identical copies of the stencil, or that it be sent to the receiver in some guise. But over-use of the card would allow a code breaker to identify where the 'windows' are, allowing instant reading of the real message. There is also a risk that the message created to 'camouflage' the hidden words may be so clumsily worded as to create suspicion.

good to know

The rotating grille
A refinement of the method is the 'turning grille' system, in which the grille is rotated through 180° or flipped every, say, nine letters. This is remarkably effective, provided the windows never overlap.

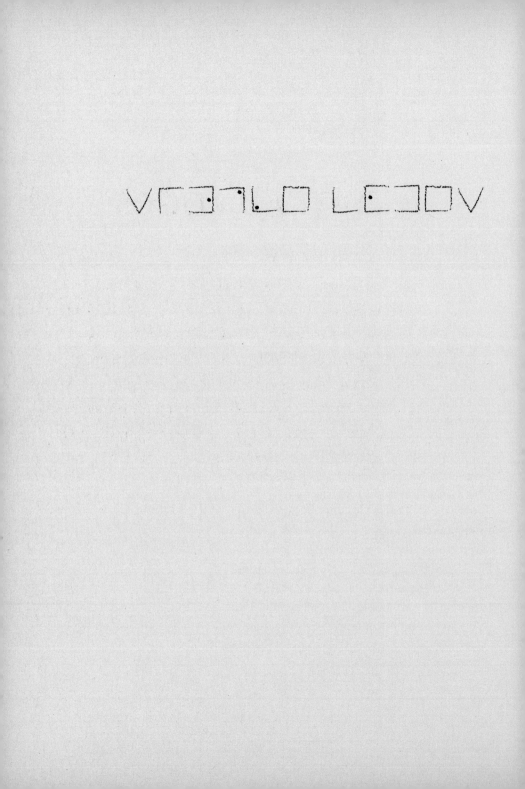

3 Simple codes

This section shows how simple codes can be
created and demonstrates how a code breaker
would go about finding the real, hidden text.
Where possible, it includes examples of how
such codes have been used in the past.
The terms 'code' and 'cipher' are often used
interchangeably, but they have slightly different
meanings (see the box on page 57).

Making simple codes and ciphers

Simple codes and ciphers can be created with pencil, paper and patience. This chapter describes various examples of simple codes, which, while being quite basic in formulation, are in fact a very effective method of concealing meaning, and have been used by secret agents and spies many times.

Spaces, books and dots

Perhaps the simplest way of concealing a written message is a space code, in which the plaintext is broken up into different 'words'. For example 'This is an example of a space code' could be encoded as THI SISA NEXAM PLEO FAS PAC ECO DE. It wouldn't fool anyone for long, though. Neither will a backwards code: EDOC SDRAWKCAB A LLIW REHTIEN. This message can be made slightly less recognizable by breaking up the word groups: EDO CSD RAWK CAB ALL IWREH TIEN.

However, it is very easy to create a code allowing you to talk or write to a friend with no chance of others understanding your communication. All you have to do is agree to change each important word for another word, rendering the plaintext incomprehensible.

A history book written in 14th-century Egypt notes that tax and army officials used the names of perfumes, fruits, birds and flowers to denote certain

good to know

Transposition ciphers

▶ A cipher in which letters are rearranged, as in the backwards cipher on this page, is known as a transposition cipher.

▶ Other examples in this chapter are the rail fence cipher on pages 64-7 and the Greek scytale (see page 64).

▶ Transposition ciphers are easy to spot if you analyze the letter frequency (see pages 82-5).

letters or terms. This kind of code is pretty much unbreakable, but there are difficulties in execution:

▶ All correspondents need a copy of the code words in use, and this document will be bulky and hard to conceal.

▶ Anyone able to see this code book can understand your messages. You would also probably need to expand the code book to allow you to use a wide vocabulary, so you would then have security issues about this valuable document.

▶ If someone studies your conversation or writing, they will be able to make informed guesses about the types of words in the gaps (verbs, nouns, numbers, etc.) and eventually decipher at least parts of it simply from the context.

Codes where words stand for other words or phrases are known as sub rosa codes. A famous story involving their use comes from World War I, when censors who were suspicious of the cable message 'Father is dead' amended it to 'Father is deceased'. This caused confusion with the recipient, who cabled back, 'Is father dead or deceased?'

The practice was also widespread among spies in World War II. A series of intercepted letters contained detailed concerns apparently about the correspondent's doll collection such as, 'A broken doll in a hula grass skirt will have all damages repaired by the first week of February.' It was eventually established that each doll referred to was code for a different American ship.

See also the null cipher on pages 48-9.

See also the null cipher on pages 48-9.

> **must know**
>
> **Codes vs ciphers**
>
> A 'code' is a system in which words and/or phrases are changed, and therefore requires a code book, which is like a dictionary. In a 'cipher', the substitution is of letters, so no code book is necessary, and deciphering requires knowledge of how the letters have been changed. As is discussed later, an advantage of ciphers is that the same letter can be changed to many different letters or numbers, making it much harder to detect (see page 88). Turning a message into code and then enciphering that text is called 'superencipherment'.

Dictionary code

One way to avoid having to create and update a code book is to use a dictionary code for all, or some, words. This has proved a popular method for secret agents countless times. When you wish to disguise a word, you quote the page, column and entry number where it appears in your dictionary: you just have to make sure both parties are using the same edition of the tome. For example, in the tenth edition of *Webster's Collegiate Dictionary*, the word 'dictionary' is on page 322, column 1, and is the third entry, so its code number is 322,1,3. The comma is required to avoid confusion between the three pieces of information: 32213 could mean page 32, column 2, entry 13, which is 'allow'. The number for 'code' is 221,2,17.

Thus the plaintext, 'This sentence is in dictionary code' would be encoded as:

'THIS SENTENCE IS IN 322,1,3 221,2,17' if you just change two key words, or if you change them all:

1227,1,14 1067,1,13 620,2,11 585,2,6 322,1,3 221,2,17

Codes in action
In the 19th-century Peninsular Wars, British forces used dictionary code for communication between different parts of the army. The code remained secure, while the British were able to break their enemy's cipher.

Breaking a dictionary code

Anyone trying to decode this message would immediately know how many words it contained by counting the spaces between numbers. The use of three numbers for each word also betrays the 'page, column, entry' format, especially as the middle number is always 1 or 2. So you would quickly discern that it is a dictionary code, but would be

unable to proceed further without identifying which
dictionary was used.

Refining the code
Armed with this knowledge, you might decide to
conceal the page numbers by making every page
number four digits, leaving the column number
untouched, but making all the entry numbers two
digits, filling in gaps with zeroes. Now you can run
all the numbers together and remove the commas:

122711410671130620211058520603221030221217

Another refinement is to use any odd number
instead of '1' to indicate the entry is in the left-hand
column, and any even number in place of '2' for the
right-hand column. This will confuse the decoder.
Yet another trick is to add the same number to every
figure. For example, adding five to each figure in the
code above would produce this ciphertext:

123261910726180625716059071103276080226722

A determined decoder will still be able to recognize
number patterns, although you can further
confound them by changing the procedure slightly
by locating the words in the same position but four
pages in front of the word in the plaintext. Now your
message reads:

THERAPEUTICS SEMESTER INVESTITURE
IMPATIENCE DEWAR CLOVE

must know

No room for erorr
Whenever you are encoding, it is crucial to avoid making any mistakes, as these will confuse the recipient of the message. This is especially true when using numbers. Inputting the wrong number or, worse, omitting a digit, will render the message incomprehensible.

The 'four pages back in the dictionary' code is exactly the method unearthed in the scandal surrounding the disputed 1876 American Presidential election in which both Democrats and Republicans were suspected of malpractice. In one Democrat message, the phrase, MINUTELY PREVIOUSLY READMIT DOLTISH, translates as, 'Must purchase Republican elector', via the *Household English Dictionary* published in 1876.

Book code

Any book can function as a code book in much the same way as a dictionary, and this again, for centuries, has been a very common encoding method. One problem, though, is in finding the words in the book in the first place. For example, a message from Benedict Arnold, the 18th-century American general who defected to the British, using this system found him culling words from pages as far apart as 35, 91 and 101. That's a lot of searching for one word – it would be infinitely easier today using the search facility on a word-processing program.

The disadvantage of using a dictionary or book for creating a code is that many words, such as place names, simply won't be in the text and will then need to be laboriously spelled out letter by letter, with the code specifying the page, line, word and letter numbers. This will create a very long message, which occupies hours for both encoder and decoder. However, provided the interceptor never identifies the book used, it is a very secure method, especially if the book is changed frequently, which explains its popularity. Another benefit is that the shelves of secret agents will not be stacked with incriminating code books or stencils, but merely hold a stock of seemingy innocent books.

A story from World War I illustrates another method of using a book code. A blank postcard was sent from Turkey to Sir Henry Jones, 184 King's Road, Tighnabruaich, Scotland. There was a Sir Henry, whose son had been taken prisoner by the Turks. The address was wrong but somehow it still reached him. On receiving the message the baffled father took it to the legendary code-breaking office Room 40 at the Admiralty (see page 153). Here a cryptanalyst called Reverend Montgomery realized that the address referred to chapter 18, verse 4 of the first book of Kings: 'Obadiah took a hundred prophets, and hid them fifty in a cave, and fed them with bread and water'. The message was reassurance for Sir Henry that his son was indeed being held prisoner but was being well treated.

The dot cipher

This is totally different to the practice of dotting or pinpricking newspapers favoured by thrifty Victorians (see page 48). The alphabet is written on squared paper with one letter on each line and the receiver needs an exact copy. The ciphertext is created by putting a dot under each letter in your message, working down the page so that each new dot is on a new line. The end result looks like piano roll music for an automatic piano. So the message, 'Dots lines and zigzags' will look like this (see over):

Dot cipher

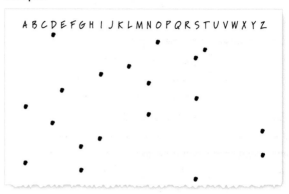

Line cipher

Zigzag cipher

The dot cipher, line cipher and zigzag cipher are natural developments of each other.

The alphabet can also be written vertically rather than horizontally in which case the dots will read from left to right.

You can disguise the message by connecting the dots to make lines, a graph or even a crazy picture, or go in sequence to create a zigzag pattern as you can see in the illustrations opposite. The dots from which these variations are produced must be positioned precisely to avoid confusion in decoding. A refinement of this system is to set the alphabet in a different, pre-arranged order, such as backwards or by writing all the vowels first.

Knot code

The zigzag cipher can, in turn, be adapted to create a message concealed in a length of wool, thread or string. If you stretch a piece of thread or string along the alphabet strip, you can mark with ink, or tie a knot, at the first letter in the message. You then stretch the thread back along the alphabet and repeat the process for the second letter, then the third, and so on. You end up with a length of string or thread that can be rolled up, used to tie a parcel or hidden in some way and so is very unlikely to attract suspicion on its travels to the recipient. This method was allegedly used for communication between British World War II prisoners and their relatives at home.

Transposition ciphers

In transposition ciphers, letters are rearranged in a different order, creating an anagram of the message. There are various systems determining how to change the position of the letters to form a cipher.

The Greek scytale

The scytale is the earliest known piece of cryptographic equipment, dating from 5th-century BC Greece. Probably first used by the Spartans to carry messages around the battlefield, it is a simple transposition machine. A piece of parchment rather like a ribbon was wrapped around a cylinder, such as a wooden staff. The message was then written unencrypted onto the coiled paper.

Once removed from the rod, the writing was just a jumble of letters that would be meaningless if the enemy captured it. It is possible that messengers wore the fabric as a belt with the writing on the inside. When the message was delivered, it was wrapped around a cylinder identical in diameter to the first one, and could be read.

Part of the scytale's value was the speed at which communication took place, because no enciphering and deciphering was involved: the message was written, transported with reasonable security, and read.

The rail fence cipher

In the 19th century, hundreds of miles of fences were put up across the US as new territories were taken over. Known as split-rail fences, they form a zigzag pattern when seen from above, similar to the pattern made by letters in the rail fence cipher. If you write the message, 'The rail fence cipher makes a zigzag pattern' in zigzags it looks like this:

```
T E A L E C C P E M K S Z G A P T E N
 \/\/\/\/\/\/\/\/\/\/\/\/\/\/\/\/\/\/
H R I F N E I H R A E A I Z G A T R
```

The enciphered message is created by writing each row, choosing, if you wish, to put the letters into groups of four, in which case you will need to fill in the gaps with 'padding letters' or 'nulls', which are usually X or Z. The first null indicates where the new line starts. In this example, the last two nulls are to ensure the ciphertext ends with a group of four letters.

TEAL ECCP EMKS ZGAP TENX HRIF NEIH RAEA IZGA TRZZ

To decipher this message, count the letters (40) then divide into two groups. You can now put the letters into order by writing the first letter from each group, then the second, and so on, ignoring the nulls, and reading the words created.

Refining the rail fence cipher
The cipher can be written in three or more rows, either zigzagging across the page or starting a new column every three letters. This is the code written in zigzag pattern for, 'A three row cipher would look like this':

```
A   E   W   H   O   L   L   T
 \ /\ /\ /\ /\ /\ /\ /\ /
T R E O C P E W U D O K I E H S
 \/ \/ \/ \/ \/ \/ \/ \/
H   R   I   R   L   O   K   I
```

This creates the code message AEWH OLLT TREO CPEW UDOK IEHS HRIR LOKI

Deciphering this rail fence cipher

The message can be revealed by writing out the eight letters of the top row, the 16 in pairs of the middle row, and the eight of the bottom row, recreating the zigzag pattern of the original. Then the letters are written out in the new order reading down and up.

Four rows

If you think of the fence posts creating a grid, you can make a four-row rail fence cipher, writing across or, in this case, down:

T	I	I	N	O
H	S	T	I	W
I	W	T	N	S
S	R	E	R	A

In blocks of five letters this would read TIINO HSTIW IWTNS SRERA. The 'A' at the end indicates a solitary null (see box, below left).

Deciphering the four-row message

The agreed key is a four-row grid, so you divide the total number of letters (20) by this to find the number of columns, which is five. You can then write it out, or, as you become more experienced, simply read every fifth letter, ignoring the solitary null. It reads 'This is written in rows'.

Breaking rail fence ciphers

Like other transposition ciphers, the cipher features letter frequencies similar to those of the language in everyday use (see pages 82–3), so you can identify them by counting letter frequency. Now you need to unscramble the letters on the page, which is much easier than finding substitutes for them. To decipher a transposition cipher you need to identify then ignore the padding nulls – frequency analysis (see pages 82–5) will help here – then try reading every second letter, and if that doesn't work, every third letter, and so on. The longer the message, the bigger the jumps will have to be.

Transposition with a key

Once the letters are put into a four-column grid, they do not have to be enciphered in the standard left to right, or top to bottom order. For example, your key could be: start at the bottom right corner and spiral clockwise to the centre. This is called a route cipher and makes decryption much more difficult. The encryption of the same four-row message already used :

T	I	I	N	O
H	S	T	I	W
I	W	T	N	S
S	R	E	R	A

would then begin at the A in the bottom right corner and read as:

ARERS IHTII NOWSN TWSTI

Other paths for enciphering include:
▶ In a spiral from the centre.
▶ Diagonally (specifying upwards or downwards, left to right or right to left).
▶ Up one column, down the next.

Number or word keys

Another way to scramble the letters from a grid is to identify the columns with a key word or number. This is called columnar transposition. If you have a four-column grid with the message, 'This makes it more complicated' written across it looks like this:

T	H	I	S
M	A	K	E
S	I	T	M
O	R	E	C
O	M	P	L
I	C	A	T
E	D	T	B

Two nulls have been added, the last being B to indicate 'two nulls'. Making the other a T rather than, say, an X makes it harder to spot as an imposter.

Instead of writing the encryption out by following the column order, you can change it with the four-letter keyword CODE (one letter for each column). In alphabetical order within the word, these letters are 1st, 2nd, 3rd and 4th. This would re-arrange the grid to read:

C	O	D	E
1st	4th	2nd	3rd
T	S	H	I
M	E	A	K
S	M	I	T
O	C	R	E
O	L	M	P
I	T	C	A
E	B	D	T

In blocks of five (with a three on the end, which could be filled with nulls if you choose), the enciphered message now reads:

TSHIM EAKSM ITOCR EOLMP ITCAE BDT

Deciphering the message

The decipherer now works out the column lengths by dividing the key length (four, from the keyword CODE) into the message length (28 letters). This reveals the number of rows as seven, so the content of each column can be identified, then re-ordered according to the code word, the nulls counted and removed, and the message read.

Double transposition

A technique for breaking down transposition ciphers is to guess the number of rows and grouping letters accordingly, then sliding the letters around looking for words or anagrams. Double transposition counteracts this by repeating the scrambling of columns during encryption, usually with a second keyword. Both keywords can be changed at will to protect the cipher from attack.

Double transposition was used by the German army during World War I, but it was successfully broken by the French. They were greatly aided by the fact that the Germans, confident of the security of their cipher, used the same key for more than a week at a time - a major sin in the world of cryptography (see page 116). Double transposition was widely used in World War II, as well, as it was regarded as the most complex cipher an agent could use as a field cipher.

must know

Polyliteral transposition
This is the trick of transposing letters in pairs, threes or other groups, even of mixing the size of the group each time. It is effective, but makes transposition even more laborious, with errors likely at both ends of the coding process.

Substitution ciphers

Transposition ciphers create anagrams of the plaintext by mixing up the words or letters. Substitution ciphers leave the letters in the order they should be read, but disguise them.

Mono to poly
▶ A substitution cipher that uses one alphabet for encryption so that each plaintext letter is represented by the same ciphertext letter throughout is described as 'monoalphabetic'.
▶ Later ciphers that used more than one alphabet are known as polyalphabetic ciphers (see pages 86–109).

Shift ciphers

An early example of this comes from 2,000 years ago in a message sent by Roman leader Julius Caesar to Cicero, whose forces were under siege. The Roman letters were substituted with Greek letters, which Caesar knew the poet and lover of the Greek language would understand.

Caesar had many reasons to encrypt his messages and did so in many ways. The most famous is the shift cipher, in which each letter is replaced by the letter three places on in the alphabet: 'a' becomes D, 'b' becomes E, 'c' is F and so on. The message, 'Named after Julius Caesar' would be written as:

QDPHG DIWHU MXOLXV FDHVDU

The Caesar shift was widely used for centuries – it was even one of the ciphers being used by Russian forces in 1915. A big advantage of the shift cipher is that it does not require a code book as the method can be easily memorized. It can also be adapted to shift the letters any number of places from 1 to 25 for a standard 26-letter alphabet through the use of a code number. This is called the St Cyr cipher, after the French national military academy where it was taught in the 1880s. However, it is also known as the slide rule cipher because it can be created by sliding an alphabet strip below an identical strip to create the shifted letters. So the code number 7 would indicate a 7-place shift, creating this alphabet:

Plain alphabet: a b c d e f g h i j k l m n o p q r s t u v w x y z
Cipher alphabet: H I J K L M N O P Q R S T U V W X Y Z A B C D E F G

Breaking the shift cipher

However, the fact that the cipher is in alphabetical order makes this kind of shift key very easy to break. All you have to do is take one word or set of letters and try out all the possible encryption keys. For example, if the cipher text includes the letters SIFBVE, the word can be discovered through the process shown in this table:

Shift	Produces letters
0	SIFBVE
1	TJGCWF
2	UKHDXG
3	VLIEYH
4	WMJFZI
5	XNKGAJ
6	YOLHBK
7	ZPMICL
8	AQNJDM
9	BROKEN

So shifting the encrypted message nine places along the alphabet solves the cipher.

must know

Early substitution
A 10th-century Persian substitution alphabet used the names of birds for letters of the alphabet. Another substituted them with names for parts of the night sky.

Using keywords

Another approach is to start the alphabet with a key word, followed by the remaining letters in alphabetical order. This allows regular changing of the cipher by replacing the keyword and enhances security of the system. Repeated letters in a code word are omitted (so omitted would be spelt with one 't' as omited). Here the keyword is 'scramble':

Plain alphabet: a b c d e f g h i j k l m n o p q r s t u v w x y z
Cipher alphabet: S C R A M B L E D F G H I J K N O P Q T U V W X Y Z

Notice that some letters stay the same in this cipher, which is best avoided. There are a couple of ways of getting around this. The cipher alphabet can follow the key word in any agreed order, so one with the keyword 'backwards', followed by the rest of the alphabet in reverse, would look like this:

Plain alphabet: a b c d e f g h i j k l m n o p q r s t u v w x y z
Cipher alphabet: B A C K W R D S Z Y X R U T Q P O N M L J I H G F E

Alternatively, the keyword need not come at the beginning of the alphabet. So if the keyword is 'thirteen' and happens to start on the 13th letter of the alphabet, you would produce this cipher alphabet:

Plain alphabet: a b c d e f g h i j k l m n o p q r s t u v w x y z
Cipher alphabet: L M O P Q S U V W X Y Z T H I R E N A B C D F G J K

Since one weakness of these substitution ciphers is their alphabetical order, the way to protect it is to put the alphabet into a different, random order. Theoretically this creates 403,291,461,126,605,635,584,000,000 different possible cipher alphabets – more than someone could test in a lifetime, even if they were equipped with a computer.

However, because the cipher alphabet is random, it would have to be memorized by two people (which is unreliable) or written down (which threatens cipher security). It is also, as we will see later, easily broken by frequency analysis.

must know

Letters to numbers
Another simple substitution cipher is the Polybius square, which converts letters to numbers and is described on pages 75-6.

Typewriter cipher

The typewriter code substitutes the alphabet for the letters of the keyboard in order from top to bottom (the qwerty keyboard is a random order for which there seems to be no explanation – it certainly doesn't reflect frequency of use for its letters. However, have you noticed that the characters of 'typewriter' are all on the top row of letters?).

Plain alphabet: a b c d e f g h i j k l m n o p q r s t u v w x y z
Typewriter alphabet: Q W E R T Y U I O P A S D F G H J K L Z X C V B N M

Alternatives are for each key to represent, say, the one to its left, with the cipher wrapping round to the beginning when the end of the row is reached, or to the left and above, so that 'typewriter cipher' would be enciphered as:

5603248534 D80Y34

More complex shift ciphers

A cipher with an alphabetical basis can be attacked fairly easily by cryptanalysts because there will be a pattern to at least parts of the cipher for the letters not in the keyword.

One option is to re-order the alphabet, for example by writing it backwards:

Plain alphabet: a b c d e f g h i j k l m n o p q r s t u v w x y z
Cipher alphabet: Z Y X W V U T S R Q P O N M L K J I H G F E D C B A

This produces one of the most famous (and simplest) ciphers in history: Atbash, a cipher in which the first letter becomes the last, the second becomes the second last, reversing the alphabetical order. This was a device used by Hebrew scribes to encipher parts of the Old Testament. ATBASH is so-called because in the cipher the Hebrew letter A becomes T, B becomes Sh, and so on, hence ATBSh, which is pronounced ATBASH. It is remarkably easy to break because there is only one solution!

Another option is to write all the vowels first, followed by the consonants:

Plain alphabet: a b c d e f g h i j k l m n o p q r s t u v w x y z
Cipher alphabet: A E I O U B C D F G H J K L M N P Q R S T V W X Y Z

Again, to prevent letters being encrypted as themselves, do this backwards:

Plain alphabet: a b c d e f g h i j k l m n o p q r s t u v w x y z
Cipher alphabet: Z Y X W V T S R Q P N M L K J H G F D C B U O I E A

If the cipher alphabet is not alphabetical at all, it is harder to break. However, both parties must remember or keep a record of the invented alphabet, which can weaken security.

Using numbers

Encrypting a word message into a number cipher is another way to disguise meaning. The most obvious way is to number the alphabet ('a' = 1, 'b' = 2, etc.), but this will be simple to detect (see frequency analysis, pages 82–5). All the variations in alphabet order described on pages 70–4 could be adapted to create a number rather than a letter alphabet.

Another way, which has more possibilities for deception, is a five-by-five grid. As there are 26 letters in the alphabet, this requires two to be combined: 'i' and 'j' will do. The grid looks like this:

	1	2	3	4	5
1	A	B	C	D	E
2	F	G	H	I/J	K
3	L	M	N	O	P
4	Q	R	S	T	U
5	V	W	X	Y	Z

Letters can now have a number created from their grid reference with the horizontal row number appearing first then the vertical column, so 'b' would be 12 and 's' would be 43. Thus the plaintext 'number cipher' would be encrypted as:

33-45-32-12-15-42 13-24-35-23-15-42

The alphabet can be written in any agreed order in the grid, perhaps using a keyword, and decryption is a simple matter of matching letters to their numbers. One disadvantage of this system is that the ciphertext is twice the length of the plaintext, and writing out the enciphered message is double the work.

The Greek square

The numbering method on such a grid is known as the Greek square, or the Polybius checkerboard, after its inventor. Dating back 2,200 years to ancient Greece, it was used to send messages long distances by holding up torches, with the number held in each hand indicating the grid reference. There are records of a similar method being used in 16th-century Armenia to add a sense of mystery to religious texts.

must know

Different alphabets
Polybius did not have to drop a letter for the five-by-five grid because at that time the Greek alphabet only had 24 letters. To work with the 33-letter Cyrillic alphabet, the square can be expanded to six-by-six – which also allows for the addition of digits to a standard alphabet.

The system lends itself to communication with lamps, smoke signals, knots or stitches in string or quilts, and sounds. Translated into a system of knocks, it is a method for messaging between prison cells. It is said to have been used in this way by captives of the Russian Tsars, and by American prisoners of war in the Vietnam War.

Breaking the Greek square
Since each letter is matched by one number, this cipher can be broken by frequency analysis (see pages 82–5) just like any other monoalphabetic substitution cipher. However, there are possibilities for making it more complex, which are explored on pages 88–90.

Using handwriting
One cipher cunningly conceals its use of the Polybius square in cursive, or joined up, handwriting. The number of characters between each break where the pen is removed creates a numeric code. Apparently this method was also used in letters home from captured German U-boat officers during World War II. Using the ciphertext given on page 75:

33-45-32-12-15-42 13-24-35-23-15-42

The message – in this case, 'Many secrets can be hidden in seemingly innocuous messages using this coding trick' – would be written as follows:

Man yse cret scanb ehi dd e ni n seemi ngly in n ocv ov smes sag esvsi ng thi s codin gtri ck

Using symbols

A different approach to substitution ciphers is to use an alternative alphabet consisting wholly or partly of symbols. This has been done many times in history. The earliest record of it is an ancient Greek practice of using dots for vowels (one for alpha, two for epsilon, and so on), with the consonants left unchanged.

An early example of this is the King Charlemagne cipher dating from the 8th century and used in his battle reports. It was a 23-letter symbolic alphabet (there was no 'j', 'v' or 'w' at the time), which recipients of his messages were required to learn.

The King Charlemagne symbol alphabet code.

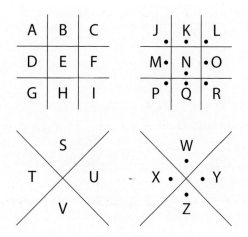

The pigpen cipher used symbols based on where the letter fell when written in grids in the way shown.

Pigpen cipher

This is an alternative alphabet that was widely used by masons in the 18th century (it is also known as the Freemason cipher), although some put its origins centuries earlier in the Crusades. The letters of the alphabet are written inside a grid (which looks like an animal pen, hence the name) (see diagrams above). Each letter is represented by the graphic symbol from its part of the grid, with dots added to allow each symbol to be used for two different letters. So 'This is pigpen cipher' would look like this:

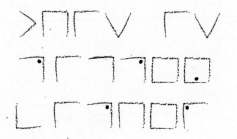

Pigpen cipher was used by Confederate forces during the American Civil War, possibly because, apparently, many of their generals were Freemasons and so were familiar with the system. It was solved by a former shop worker who recognized the symbols because the same system had been used to mark the prices of goods in the shop he had worked in before the war!

A variant of the pigpen cipher (also based on a grid), but with the same shape now representing one of three letters, which are identified by placing a dot on the left, centre or right, is known as the Rosicrucian cipher.

The Rosicrucian cipher is a development of the pigpen cipher. Dots denote which of the three possible letters is being represented.

ABC	DEF	GHI
JKL	MNO	PQR
STU	VWX	YZ

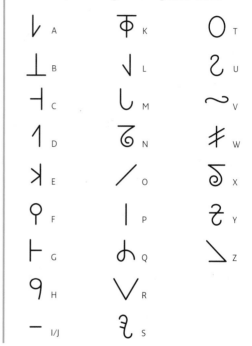

Death by substitution

When Mary, Queen of Scots was being held at
Chartley Hall in Staffordshire in 1586, she knew that
letters in and out would be read for indications of
any plot against her half-sister Queen Elizabeth I.
Consequently, when she wanted to correspond with
a Catholic sympathizer, she took precautions:

▶ Letters were smuggled in and out hidden in the bung hole of beer kegs.

▶ She wrote using 23 letter substitutions and 36 code signs for words and phrases. This blend of code words and cipher is known as a nomenclator.

▶ She avoided direct references to plots to kill the queen and put her on the throne.

Mary was confident that these precautions prevented her being accused of treason. She did not know that:

▶ Her correspondent Gilbert Clifford was a double agent.

▶ Even the brewer who supplied the beer kegs was in the pay of English spymaster Francis Walsingham.

▶ Her letters were routinely opened and copied for analysis.

▶ Once Mary's nomenclator was broken, Walsingham was browsing through her letters before her servants sneaked them past the guards at Chartley Hall.

Such was Walsingham's grasp of the intricacies of Mary's code system that he even had extra writing forged onto one of her own letters to try to elicit incriminating information. Although she denied all at her trial, Mary's letters showed she knew and approved of a plot against Elizabeth. It was enough for her to be executed.

The queen's spymaster had set up a cipher school in London, where Mary's code was broken. The method relied on a revolutionary new weapon in western cryptanalysis: frequency analysis.

Frequency analysis

Frequency analysis is the deadly weapon that breaks substitution and transposition ciphers. It was first developed in the 9th century by an Arab religious scholar called Al-Kindi, studying sacred texts of previous civilizations. He realized that in any language some letters are used far more often than others, that some only appear rarely, and that this pattern remains consistent.

must know

From E to Z

▶ In the English language, about one in every eight letters is likely to be an 'e'. So, if about one-eighth of the letters in a ciphertext are Y, it is likely to be an 'e' in plaintext.

▶ The vowels, a, e, i, o and u, and the part-time vowel 'y', make up about 40 per cent of English text.

▶ The least common letters are k, j, q, x and z, which, between them, account for just over one per cent of English letters used.

Therefore, in a substitution cipher, the most commonly occurring ciphertext letters are likely to represent the most common letters in the plaintext language. This allows cryptanalysts to make informed guesses about the identity of individual letters following statistical analysis of both the plaintext language and the ciphertext. Furthermore, once a common letter is known, its position in a word helps identify its partners. For example, once 'e' is identified, any three-letter words with which it ends are very likely to be 'the', so identifying 't' and 'h'.

Common letters

In order of frequency, the English alphabet reads:

▶ e, t, a, o, n, l, s, r, h, l, d, c, u, f, p, m, w, y, b, g, v, k, x, q, j, z.

▶ Counting the letters in the plaintext, if the six most common letters are the first six listed here, and there are very few of the final letters listed, the cipher is likely to be a giant anagram created by transposition.

▶ By similar logic, if the most frequently occurring letters in the ciphertext are those that only appear rarely in natural text, the cipher is likely to be of the substitution variety.

The next step is to look for short words. Only 'A' and 'I' are one-letter words, but there are many more of two, three and four letters. If you can identify word lengths, either because they are not disguised or by identifying the spacer null letter, you can guess what they are most likely to be according to their natural frequency of use and the context (some words are unlikely to follow others, or to start or end sentences). It is worth bearing in mind, however, that code messages do not always follow the rules of sense and grammar. Ciphertext may be shortened to save effort in translating and transmission, and may include code words that are short for phrases or sensitive information.

However, frequency tables are gold dust for a cryptanalyst. For example, it is much easier to make informed guesses about the ends of words when armed with the information that more than half of all words end with e, s, t or d. Similarly, if two letters in a transposition ciphertext are the same, they are most likely to be (in order): ss, ee, tt, ff, ll, mm, oo. Two letters in a substitution ciphertext may or may not be the same.

The brain is a powerful tool and is very good at filling in gaps. For example:

-ou a-e -roba-ly ab-e t- rea- t-is te— e-en tho—- a -ot — it i- m—si-g!

This shows how finding some letters, even in a shifting substitution text, can allow you to identify new information.

did you know?

Morse sense
The dots and dashes used in Morse code were decided according to frequency analysis, with the most commonly used letters requiring the least effort to transmit (see pages 32–4).

must know

Know the context
There are also tables for the most common words used in scientific, religious and other fields. If you know who the message is from, and its likely subject area, these are invaluable.

must know

Double value	Triple knowledge	Four-letter words
The most common two-letter words in English are:	The most common three-letter words in English are:	The most common four-letter words in English are:
1 of	1 the	1 that
2 to	2 and	2 with
3 in	3 for	3 have
4 it	4 are	4 this
5 is	5 but	5 will
6 be	6 not	6 your
7 as	7 had	7 from
8 at	8 her	8 they
9 so	9 was	9 know
10 we	10 one	10 want
11 he	11 our	11 been
12 by	12 out	12 good
13 or	13 you	13 much
14 on	14 all	14 some
15 do	15 any	15 time
16 if	16 can	16 very
17 me	17 day	17 when
18 my	18 get	18 come
19 up	19 has	19 here
20 an	20 him	20 just

must know

A void

One text that would perplex a frequency analyst is *La Disparition* by Georges Perec, translated from French to English as *A Void* by Gilbert Adair. There is not a single letter 'e' in the entire 300-page novel in either version.

Digraphs

A digraph is two letters that together make a single sound. These are common in English, which helps in cryptanalysis because identifying one letter leads us towards the other. In order of frequency they are:

▶ th, he, an, in, er, on, re, ed, nd, ha, at, en, es, of, nt, ea, ti, to, io, le, is, ou, ar, as, de, rt, ve.

Trigraphs are parts of words formed by three letters. Their order of frequency is:

▶ the, and, tha, ent, ion, tio, for, nde, has, nce, tis, oft, men.

Other languages

Since many intercepted messages are from foreign agents, cryptanalysts must gather frequency data on other languages. The most common letters in some other European languages are:

- ▶ French: e, n, i, r, s.
- ▶ German: e, a, i, s, t.
- ▶ Italian: e, a, i o, n.
- ▶ Spanish: e, a, i, s, n.

Letter knowledge

Word breaks are valuable to a cryptanalyst because they can gain clues using the following information:

- ▶ Most common first letter in a word, in order:

t, o, a, w, b, c, d, s, f, m, r, h, i, y, e, g, l, n, o, u, j, k.

- ▶ Most common third letter in a word, in order:

e, s, a, r, n, i.

- ▶ Most common last letter in a word, in order:

e, s, t, d, n, r, y, f, l, o, g, h, a, k, m, p, u, w.

- ▶ Letters most likely to follow the letter 'e':

r, s, n, d.

Word frequency

Zipf's law identifies the most common words and in what proportion of text they will appear. Named after Harvard linguist George Kingsley Zipf, it shows that 7 per cent of all words are 'the', followed by 'of' at about half that frequency, then 'and'. Cryptanalysts can apply this law to make informed guesses about words in context.

must know

From East to West
The man credited with bringing Arab knowledge of frequency analysis to the West was Leon Battista Alberti (1404–72), the greatest cryptographer of his day and the first man to suggest superencipherment (see page 57). Experienced cryptographers equipped with information on frequency data can solve codes in languages they cannot even read.

WESOHBXHRLJPS
JYWXLHZ

4 Polyalphabetic ciphers

After centuries when governments and armies were reasonably confident in the security of substitution ciphers, they realized in the 16th century that more complex codes were needed if their secrets were to stay that way.

Beating frequency analysis

The spread in the use of frequency analysis stimulated cryptographers to create ciphers or codes that defied it. There was enormous pressure to do this as nations continued to fight, trade and negotiate with each other, and there was a clear need for secure communication within governments and armies.

Adding to the Greek square

In a null cipher, a message is hidden inside the plaintext (see page 48). However, another way to use nulls is to adapt the Greek square system outlined on page 75. This allocates each of 25 letters (with two doubling-up) a two-digit number, which is actually a grid reference.

	1	2	3	4	5
1	A	B	C	D	E
2	F	G	H	I/J	K
3	L	M	N	O	P
4	Q	R	S	T	U
5	V	W	X	Y	Z

Making the grid bigger creates more boxes to put letters in. This enables the encoder to have the same letter represented by more than one number, which protects it from frequency analysis.

For example, increasing the grid from five-by-five to six-by-six creates an extra 11 boxes. These can be randomly filled with the five most common letters used in the English language: e, t, a, o and n (twice), with the final gap filled by another 'e' as it is by far the highest frequency letter at 12.7 per cent of all text. Now there are four numbers for 'e': 11, 12, 21 and 26, and three numbers each for t, a, o and n. Someone who intercepts the message and counts repeated numbers looking for 'e' will be totally misled.

	1	2	3	4	5	6
1	E	E	T	A	O	N
2	E	A	B	C	D	E
3	T	F	G	H	I/J	K
4	A	L	M	N	O	P
5	O	Q	R	S	T	U
6	N	V	W	X	Y	Z

The message 'Even trees hide secrets' has seven 'e's, which stand out very clearly as the number 15 in this message enciphered from the five-by-five grid:

15⁻51⁻15⁻33 44⁻42⁻15⁻15⁻43 23⁻24⁻14⁻15 43⁻15⁻13⁻42⁻15⁻44⁻43

A decoder would immediately start to decipher the message as:

E-51-E-33 44-42-E-E-43 23-24-14-E 43-E-13-42-E-44-43

Four-letter words with E as the first and third letters are:

eden, eked, ekes, epee, erev, even, ever, eves, ewer, ewes, exec, exes, eyed, eyer, eyes

which gives the code breaker some idea of numbers for other letters, and the beginnings of a context for the whole message.

The same message encrypted from the six-by-six grid reads as follows:

11⁻62⁻12⁻44 13⁻53⁻21⁻26⁻54 34⁻35⁻25⁻11 54⁻12⁻24⁻53⁻21⁻31⁻54

Here five numbers appear twice: 11, 12, 21, 53 and 54. While this is helpful to a code breaker, it does not give anywhere near as much information as the version encrypted on the five-by-five grid.

The great Paris cipher

Numbers were the basis of the great Paris cipher used by Napoleon's French army during the Peninsular Wars (1808–14). The French first used the Army of Portugal code, which grew from 50 to 150 numbers, each giving a short instruction. Wellington's self-trained cryptanalyst George Scovell cracked this, but was initially confounded by a new cipher introduced in 1811. This eventually used 1,400 numbers, including more than 130 for 'e' alone to combat frequency analysis. Other tricks used were:

▶ Adding meaningless figures to the ends of words (cryptanalysts study beginnings and ends of words first, looking for patterns).

▶ Disguising standard phrases by adding meaningless numbers (see cribs, pages 115–17).

However, for ease of use and to save space, the French only enciphered key words, leaving the rest as plaintext (also known as *en clair*). So a typical message would read (in English): 'In the letter of 16 March 1207 announced 607.73.432.1181.192.1077.600.530.497.701.711.700 that he considers appropriate.'

This allowed Scovell, a fine linguist, to discern the context of the enciphered words and phrases, so that he could make more informed guesses and follow up these hunches. Additionally, as each number represented one letter, Scovell could discount any guesses with the wrong number of letters. It remained a formidable task, but after about a year he had cracked most of the cipher and the information he passed on to Wellington, when combined with other intelligence, was crucial in the final victory over the French at Vitoria in 1813 (although Wellington subsequently barely acknowledged it).

Expanding the alphabet

Expanding the cipher alphabet to conceal the frequency of letters is particularly effective if the ciphertext is written as numbers. If the alphabet is written out but the six most frequent letters (a, e, n, o, r, t) doubled-up and each character given a number, it would look like this:

a	a	b	c	d	e	e	f	g	h	i	j	k	l	m	n
01	02	03	04	05	06	07	08	09	10	11	12	13	14	15	16

n	o	o	p	q	r	r	s	t	t	u	v	w	x	y	z
17	18	19	20	21	22	23	24	25	26	27	28	29	30	31	32

You could repeat any letter as many times as you like, creating more 'e's, for example, and the numbers can be adjusted so that consecutive numbers do not describe the same letter – which would be a major giveaway to the cryptanalyst.

An expanded alphabet that accurately reflects the letter frequency pattern, with numbers generated at random, would look like the table on the following page:

Numbers allocated at random according to letter frequency

a	b	c	d	e	f	g	h	i	j	k	l	m
02	78	89	99	12	68	53	11	77	01	79	18	34
08	91	00	21	80	33	22	85	61			29	84
97		94	09	28			90	26			75	
72			98	52			18	31			60	
50				67			10	82				
62				87			25	47				
51				32								
92				96								
				17								
				48								
				14								
				83								

n	o	p	q	r	s	t	u	v	w	x	y	z
13	24	35	38	41	44	37	46	27	58	40	36	76
45	06	49		03	57	66	55		05		86	
16	23			64	70	42	15					
74	88			39	19	43						
63	65			73	95	56						
20	69			04	71	93						
	30					54						
						59						
						07						

One hundred numbers have been used in this table, so the number of code numbers given to each letter matches its percentage of usage in everyday language. For example, as more than 12 per cent of all letters are 'e's, so it has 12 numbers, while j, q, v, y and z all score under 1 per cent so only get one letter. This method completely nullifies attack by frequency analysis, but there are other ways to attack such ciphers.

A glimmer of hope for decoders

When trying to break this cipher, the decoder knows that each number can only represent one letter. Once identified, that number will always reveal the presence of the same letter. This can provide clues. For example, if the decipherer was fortunate enough to identify the cipher for 'q', this would suggest that the next letter must be 'u'. Similarly, a three-letter word beginning with 'a' is quite likely to be 'and'. Common two-, three- and four-letter words are listed on page 84. Other spelling-related facts include:

▶ The high-frequency vowels a, i and o are rarely seen together.

▶ The most common vowel digraph is 'ea'.

▶ The most common repeated letters are: ss, ee, tt, ff, ll, mm and oo.

▶ The pairing 'th' is common, 'ht' is not.

▶ Indeed, 'th' is the most common letter pair, followed by: he, an, in, er, re and es (see also page 84).

▶ Words are most likely to start with (top five in order): t, o, a, w, b.

▶ Words are most likely to end with (top five in order): e, s, t, d, n.

So the decoder may feel that the rules of spelling and grammar are on their side.

Swch tht lgt ff

The answer to this weakness is not to follow the rules of spelling and grammar. It's a fair bet that you can read this heading, even though the vowels and some consonants have been removed, without leaving a gap. The human brain is remarkably good at reading text like this (just look at phone texting codes, see page 37), using a mixture of word recognition and context to make sense of it. Indeed, we are able to read words with jumbled letters quite easily, *pivoredd the fsrit and lsat lttrees are in pclae*. So a plaintext that breaks spelling rules will be comprehensible to the rightful decoder, but will offer fewer clues to the interceptor.

must know

Scrt wrtng
Writing using consonants only was one of several methods of 'secret writing' suggested by English monk Roger Bacon in the 13th century.

Using more than one cipher alphabet

The breakthrough against frequency analysis was first suggested by Leon Alberti, an archetypal 15th-century Italian Renaissance man: painter, poet, linguist, philosopher, musician, architect ... and cryptographer.

Using two ciphers

Alberti realized that frequency analysis only works against a monoalphabetic cipher, so his suggestion was to use two ciphers. It would work like this:

Plain alphabet:	a b c d e f g h i j k l m n o p q r s t u v w x y z
1st cipher alphabet:	H I J K L M N O P Q R S T U V W X Y Z A B C D E F G
2nd cipher alphabet:	Q R S T U V W X Y Z A B C D E F G H I J K L M N O P

Letters of the plaintext message would be enciphered by using the two different ciphers alternately, so, for example, from the table above an alphabet ciphertext would read:

H R J T L V N X P Z R B T D V F X H Z J B L D N F P

He refined this idea with the cipher disc, a pair of copper wheels each inscribed with the alphabet. When one disc is turned, it creates a simple substitution cipher. Alberti's breakthrough was to suggest that with every few words the wheel would be turned, changing the cipher alphabet. This would be signalled to the decoder with a capital letter in the ciphertext, indicating a new position for the wheel. Thus the encrypter has a choice of 26 alphabets and can switch between them, making unwanted deciphering very difficult. Alberti's thinking was centuries ahead of its time and his invention was not widely adopted.

Using keywords

One of the many coding systems used in the American Revolutionary War employed a keyword to create several alphabets that were used concurrently. It was created by James Lovell. The word 'key' provides the key here (it could, of course, be a longer word – names were popular, because they are so memorable) and from each letter of the word the alphabet is continued. The sender then simply works across the columns to encrypt the message. So the plaintext 'Lovell' would become the ciphertext 2, 11, 24, 21, 8, 14.

1	K	E	Y
2	L	F	Z
3	M	G	A
4	N	H	B
5	O	I	C
6	P	J	D
7	Q	K	E
8	R	L	F
9	S	M	G
10	T	N	H
11	U	O	I
12	V	P	J
13	W	Q	K
14	X	R	L
15	Y	S	M
16	Z	T	N
17	A	U	O
18	B	V	P
19	C	W	Q
20	D	X	R
21	E	Y	S
22	F	Z	T
23	G	A	U
24	H	B	V
25	I	C	W
26	J	D	X

The Vigenère square

The Vigenère square takes multi-alphabets one step further by setting out the alphabet 26 times, each moved by successive shifts of one place, as shown below.

The Vigenère square (a-m)

	a	b	c	d	e	f	g	h	i	j	k	l	m
1	B	C	D	E	F	G	H	I	J	K	L	M	N
2	C	D	E	F	G	H	I	J	K	L	M	N	O
3	D	E	F	G	H	I	J	K	L	M	N	O	P
4	E	F	G	H	I	J	K	L	M	N	O	P	Q
5	F	G	H	I	J	K	L	M	N	O	P	Q	R
6	G	H	I	J	K	L	M	N	O	P	Q	R	S
7	H	I	J	K	L	M	N	O	P	Q	R	S	T
8	I	J	K	L	M	N	O	P	Q	R	S	T	U
9	J	K	L	M	N	O	P	Q	R	S	T	U	V
10	K	L	M	N	O	P	Q	R	S	T	U	V	W
11	L	M	N	O	P	Q	R	S	T	U	V	W	X
12	M	N	O	P	Q	R	S	T	U	V	W	X	Y
13	N	O	P	Q	R	S	T	U	V	W	X	Y	Z
14	O	P	Q	R	S	T	U	V	W	X	Y	Z	A
15	P	Q	R	S	T	U	V	W	X	Y	Z	A	B
16	Q	R	S	T	U	V	W	X	Y	Z	A	B	C
17	R	S	T	U	V	W	X	Y	Z	A	B	C	D
18	S	T	U	V	W	X	Y	Z	A	B	C	D	E
19	T	U	V	W	X	Y	Z	A	B	C	D	E	F
20	U	V	W	X	Y	Z	A	B	C	D	E	F	G
21	V	W	X	Y	Z	A	B	C	D	E	F	G	H
22	W	X	Y	Z	A	B	C	D	E	F	G	H	I
23	X	Y	Z	A	B	C	D	E	F	G	H	I	J
24	Y	Z	A	B	C	D	E	F	G	H	I	J	K
25	Z	A	B	C	D	E	F	G	H	I	J	K	L
26	A	B	C	D	E	F	G	H	I	J	K	L	M

This means that 't', the second most common letter, at 9 per cent frequency, is ciphered as W after three shifts (like the Ceasar alphabet), D on 10 and O on 20. The question for the encoder is how to show

The Vigenère square (n-z)

	n	o	p	q	r	s	t	u	v	w	x	y	z
1	O	P	Q	R	S	T	U	V	W	X	Y	Z	A
2	P	Q	R	S	T	U	V	W	X	Y	Z	A	B
3	Q	R	S	T	U	V	W	X	Y	Z	A	B	C
4	R	S	T	U	V	W	X	Y	Z	A	B	C	D
5	S	T	U	V	W	X	Y	Z	A	B	C	D	E
6	T	U	V	W	X	Y	Z	A	B	C	D	E	F
7	U	V	W	X	Y	Z	A	B	C	D	E	F	G
8	V	W	X	Y	Z	A	B	C	D	E	F	G	H
9	W	X	Y	Z	A	B	C	D	E	F	G	H	I
10	X	Y	Z	A	B	C	D	E	F	G	H	I	J
11	Y	Z	A	B	C	D	E	F	G	H	I	J	K
12	Z	A	B	C	D	E	F	G	H	I	J	K	L
13	A	B	C	D	E	F	G	H	I	J	K	L	M
14	B	C	D	E	F	G	H	I	J	K	L	M	N
15	C	D	E	F	G	H	I	J	K	L	M	N	O
16	D	E	F	G	H	I	J	K	L	M	N	O	P
17	E	F	G	H	I	J	K	L	M	N	O	P	Q
18	F	G	H	I	J	K	L	M	N	O	P	Q	R
19	G	H	I	J	K	L	M	N	O	P	Q	R	S
20	H	I	J	K	L	M	N	O	P	Q	R	S	T
21	I	J	K	L	M	N	O	P	Q	R	S	T	U
22	J	K	L	M	N	O	P	Q	R	S	T	U	V
23	K	L	M	N	O	P	Q	R	S	T	U	V	W
24	L	M	N	O	P	Q	R	S	T	U	V	W	X
25	M	N	O	P	Q	R	S	T	U	V	W	X	Y
26	N	O	P	Q	R	S	T	U	V	W	X	Y	Z

Square facts

The square that carries his name was devised by Blaise de Vigenère (1523–96), but relied on the discoveries of Alberti and two other cryptologists: a German monk born in 1462 called Johannes Trithemius; and Giovanni Porta, an Italian scientist born in 1535. Some claim the Vigenère square was, in fact, first devised by Giovan Batista Belaso in 1553.

which row was used for each letter. One answer is the date shift cipher.

Date shift ciphers

In the date shift cipher, the encoder might use the date of the message, a birthday or a famous date in history to determine how a message is to be enciphered. For example, take the date of the Gunpowder Plot, 5 November 1605. Numerically, this is represented as 5/11/1605, producing a code number that is written repeatedly above the plaintext. Each letter is shifted by the number of places indicated by the number above it.

Key number:	511	1605	51	116	055111605	5111
Plaintext:	The	date	of	the	gunpowder	plot
Cipher text:	YIF	EGTJ	TG	UIK	GZSQPXJEW	UMPU

Deciphering polyalphabetic ciphers using word breaks

The ciphertext of this message shows the number of words and their length. In this case the gaps reveal that there are six words: one of two letters, two of three letters, two of four letters, and one of nine. There are a limited number of words of two or three letters in any language, and sometimes these can be deduced from their context. For example, the three-letter word that begins the message is very likely to be 'The', as it so often starts sentences. The most common two-letter word is 'of', and here the two-letter word is followed by a three-letter word. Guessing that we have identified 'of', and studying the list of most common three-letter words (see page 84) in context, removing those that would not make sense, there are only five sensible possibilities: the, her, one, our, all. So by informed guesswork and without even investigating the letters themselves, it already now reads:

The EGTJ of the/her/one/our/all GZSQPXJEW UMPU.

Hiding word breaks

The standard way to conceal word breaks is to write the encrypted message in blocks of five letters. This practice seems to have been introduced by the telegraph operators of the 19th century as it made it easier to transmit nonsensical messages (code was used a lot in telegrams to cut costs).

Another way the encrypter can avoid the problem is by merging all the letters so that there are no spaces. However, this could, on occasion, cause confusion in the deciphered message, as there may be more than one interpretation of where new words begin. Instead, they could use one letter as a space indicator. Using Z in this way, the message reads:

YIFZEGTJZTGZUIKZGZSQPXJEWZUMPU

This disguises the word breaks (although the frequent occurrence of the Z gives a clue as to its role). It also requires the decipherer to make informed guesses as to when Z is working as a cipher letter and when it is a space indicator.

More ways to use the Vigenère square

Another way to use the Vigenère square is to use a keyword such as, well, 'keyword'. Taking the number of each letter's place in the alphabet, this would give following values:

K	E	Y	W	O	R	D
11	5	25	23	15	18	4

If this is written repeatedly over the plaintext it means the ciphering system is now on a cycle of seven different shifts. So the message, 'This would be very hard to decipher' is processed like this:

	K	E	Y	W	O	R	D	K	E	Y	W	O	R	D	K	E	Y	W	O	R	D	K	E	Y	W	O	R	D	K
Shift	11	5	25	23	15	18	4	11	5	25	23	15	18	4	11	5	25	23	15	18	4	11	5	25	23	15	18	4	11
Plaintext	t	h	i	s	w	o	u	l	d	b	e	v	e	r	y	h	a	r	d	t	o	d	e	c	i	p	h	e	r
Ciphertext	E	M	H	P	L	G	Y	W	I	A	B	K	W	V	J	M	Z	O	S	L	S	O	J	B	F	E	Z	I	C

In this example, the 'e' is enciphered as B, W, J and I. For the decipherer equipped with the correct keyword this is no problem: they simply shift each letter back by the indicated number of places. But for anyone trying to break the cipher without knowledge of the key (which could be a date or keyword), they will not be able to deduce an alphabetical pattern and frequency analysis will yield no clues. The cipher's main advantage is that the same letter or numbers can represent more than one letter in the plaintext alphabet – a decoder's nightmare. The keyword system is the mechanism by which the Vigenère cipher is most used and it remains a popular code among cryptology enthusiasts.

did you know?

Wind and wonderland
Both writer Lewis Carroll and inventor of the wind-measurement scale, Sir Francis Beaufort, created their own variations of the Vigenère square.

How do you break Vigenère?
The simple answer, of course, is to find the keyword.
▶ If subterfuge does not provide this, sometimes guesswork can (there is a story from World War I of cryptologists trying to find a keyword used in a

cipher created using a mechanical device correctly guessing that the word was 'machine').

▶ However, if that fails, the next option is to look for patterns in sequences that will eventually reveal how many different shifts are evident, and from this, the length of the keyword. For example, common words like 'the' or 'and' and common letter strings like 'ing' or 'ted' will appear many times in a message, so may have been encrypted the same way at some stage in a long communication. Identifying how and when this occurs allows the cryptanalyst to identify how long the keyword is.

▶ Once you know that the keyword is, say, eight letters long, you can use frequency analysis for every eighth letter, knowing all are likely to come from the same row of the Vigenère square.

▶ From this you can begin to identify letters of the keyword itself.

So breaking the Vigenère cipher is time-consuming, but possible, and is easier if messages are long, providing more ciphertext to study, or keywords are short, reducing the scrambling of letters and making patterns more discernible.

must know

A long wait
Although published in 1586, the Vigenère square was largely ignored for 200 years, after which it was widely used because it was thought impossible to break (it was known as *le chiffre indéchiffrable*). One of the people who worked out how to decipher it, in the 19th century, was Charles Babbage, father of the computer.

Ciphers using letter pairs

The Vigenère square was partly developed out of a cipher system that used the same-size grid but was inspired by the concept of disguising letters in pairs (known as 'bigrams'). Invented by Italian scholar Giavanni Porta in 1563, this was the first known polygraphic substitution cipher. It involved creating a 26 x 26 matrix with 676 cells. The alphabet was written horizontally and vertically around the matrix,

must know

Short changed
Confederate forces in the American Civil War used the Vigenère square, but their messages were easily broken because they used short keywords, which they rarely changed.

and each cell contained a symbol. The symbol in the cell that lined up with two letters became their cipher. Numbers can be used just as well as symbols, but even so, the effort required to encode and decode (which required a list of 676 cipher equivalents) was immense.

For help with cracking a bigram cipher, see the information on page 105.

The uncrackable cipher

The keyword is the weak spot of a transposition cipher because once its length has been guessed, it can be decrypted. The answer to is to have a key the same length as the plaintext, known as the running key because it runs on rather than repeats. The running key can be any text of sufficient length and all that needs to be agreed between the communicating parties is the starting point. A rather neat development of this is the use of an 'autokey'. Here, the start of the message is enciphered with a keyword, after which the revealed plaintext forms the running key to the remainder of the message.

Breaking the running key

The disadvantage of using a readable text as the key is that it will follow the conventions of grammar, and therefore of word and letter frequency. Since the most common three-letter word is 'the', the ciphertext can be attacked by assuming that the key is repeated use of 'the', which will eventually yield clues to the message.

The one-time pad

The solution to this weakness is the one-time pad: a set of randomly produced letters that reads like total gibberish. The system was devised by Gilbert S. Vernam and Joseph Mauborgne in 1918 and is also known as the Vernam cipher. Random letters are printed onto a pad, used to encipher the message, then the sheet is peeled away and destroyed. This creates a genuinely unbreakable cipher, because every letter has been generated at random so there will be no pattern to the key. The drawback is that the decrypter needs a copy of the random key, so, as with codes, anyone on the communication network has a copy of it. Therefore, someone needs to create a set of 'one-time pads' (and it is surprisingly difficult for humans to create random letters), print and distribute them and keep them safe – a logistical problem that prevents this uncrackable Vigenère cipher from being used on more than rare occasions.

The Soviet Union used one-time pad ciphers for diplomatic communication in the 1940s. The messages were intercepted and analyzed at great length by American and British cryptanalysts who discovered to their amazement that some one-time pad sheets had been re-used, allowing a proportion of the ciphers to be broken. The significance of these so-called Venona Papers is not clear, but reveals the extent to which governments are prepared to use code breaking in order to keep track of the activities of other countries.

must know

How random is random? Creating random letters or numbers is harder than you think. Imagine trying it with a keyboard: you are very likely to alternate pressing keys with your left and right hands, establishing some form of pattern. Some of the ways to generate random data include:
▶ Geiger counter emissions.
▶ Radio or other electronic 'white noise'.
▶ A lottery-style draw of balls from a tub.
▶ Measuring cosmic rays from the sun.
▶ Using a computer (although apparently this is not effective as computers use patterns).

Checkerboard ciphers

Checkerboard ciphers is a collective term for ciphers produced using the principle of the Polybius or Greek square (see page 75), in which letters are set out on a grid for encryption.

The Playfair cipher

The Playfair cipher is a highly efficient method for digraphic substitution. Instead of the 26 x 26 square of the Porta cipher (see pages 101–2), it just requires a five-by-five square containing a keyword followed by the alphabet with one letter omitted (usually 'j' but sometimes 'q'). So using the keyword 'playfair cipher', which with repeated letters left out becomes PLAYFIRCHE, the square would look like this:

P	L	A	Y	F
I	R	C	H	E
B	D	G	K	M
N	O	Q	S	T
U	V	W	X	Z

Messages are enciphered in pairs of letters following these rules:

▶ For letters not in the same row or column, the first is replaced by the letter in the same row and column as the second. The other is substituted by the letter on the same row and column as the first. The four letters thus form a rectangle, which makes the encoding process fast and easy. So in the square shown, OK would be SD.

▶ Letters on the same row are replaced by the letter to their right, with the row 'wrapping round' to the start. So 'pl' would become LA.

Why not Wheatstone?
Invented in 1854, the Playfair cipher is named after the man who promoted it, Baron Lyon Playfair. He helped to overcome initial concerns that it was too complicated to use, and it was employed by Lawrence of Arabia, British forces in the Boer War and World War I and the Australian navy during World War II.

▶ Letters in the same column are substituted by the letter that lies immediately below. So 'lr' would become RD.

▶ If a pair is formed by the same letter (i.e. 'ee') the letters are separated by a dummy 'null' letter, such as X or Z, or, in some variants, the second one is changed to X or Z.

▶ A single letter at the end of the message is made into a pair using a null such as X or Z.

For example, the surname of the inventor of this cipher, Charles Wheatstone, would become first WH EA TS TO NE, then XC CF NT NQ TI.

Breaking bigram ciphers

Messages created with the Porta and Playfair ciphers can be broken by a form of frequency analysis, since certain pairs of letters (digraphs) occur far more often than others (for example, 'qu' – see more on this on page 84), and many others never appear consecutively. However this method takes far longer than analyzing single-letter ciphers as there are 676 possible letter combinations to count.

The bifid cipher

The Playfair cipher is easy to use and can be adapted into number form, allowing a fiendish twist in the form of the bifid cipher.

must know

A fatal flaw
A major weakness of the Playfair system is that it can be used against itself because when a plaintext digraph is reversed, so is its cipher equivalent. So if 'st' gives GH, then 'ts' will give HG.

	1	2	3	4	5
1	P	L	A	Y	F
2	I	R	C	H	E
3	B	D	G	K	M
4	N	O	Q	S	T
5	U	V	W	X	Z

As an example, the name of this cipher's 1901 creator, Felix Delastelle, is enciphered using the same alphabet grid as that on the last page (although it can just be a mixed alphabet). Each letter is given a grid reference, but these are written vertically, rather than horizontally.

f	e	l	i	x	d	e	l	a	s	t	e	l	l	e
1	2	1	2	5	3	2	1	1	4	4	2	1	1	2
5	5	2	1	4	2	5	2	3	4	5	5	2	2	5

The numbers are then read going across the rows, rather than down, and put into standard five-digit groups:
12125 32114 42112 55214 25234 55225

This process is called fractionation and in itself creates a tricky cipher, but to make life for the unwelcome decoder even harder, the numbers are then used as grid references and the cipher returned to text:

12	12	53	21	14	42	11	25	52	14	25	23	45	52	25
L	L	W	I	Y	O	P	E	V	Y	E	C	T	V	E

So the ciphertext is finally broken up into fixed lengths (called periods), resulting in:

LLWIY OPEVY ECTVE

The trifid cipher

The bifid cipher works, like all pencil and paper methods, in two dimensions, but it is the father of an unusual 'three-dimensional' system called the trifid cipher. Imagine three layers of three-by-three Polybius squares on top of each other, which form a cube with a mixed alphabet.

Layer one

	1	2	3
1	M	J	S
2	Z	Q	H
3	F	O	X

Layer two

	1	2	3
1	B	T	K
2	D	Y	G
3	W	V	.

Layer three

	1	2	3
1	A	L	N
2	E	P	C
3	R	U	I

Now each letter can be given a three-digit number from its layer, row and column. For example:

T = 212

R = 331

I = 333

F = 131

D = 221

The next stage is:

t	r	i	f	i	d	s	y	s	t	e	m
2	3	3	1	3	2	1	2	1	2	3	1
1	3	3	3	3	2	1	2	1	1	2	1
2	1	3	1	3	1	3	2	3	2	1	1

This creates:

233	132	121	231	133	332	121	121	213	131	323	211
.	O	Z	W	X	U	Z	Z	K	F	C	B

So the message sent is:

.OZWXUZZKFCB

which is decoded by reversing the whole process.

The straddling checkerboard

This is a code that was used by Russian spies in the early part of the 20th century, although it was first employed 400 years previously in papal ciphers.

	0	9	8	7	6	5	4	3	2	1
	E	T	A	O	N	I	S	R		
1	B	C	D	F	G	H	J	K	L	M
2	P	Q	U	V	W	X	Y	Z	.	/

Eight letters (in this case the most common ones, but it could be a keyword or a random choice) are given single digit values (for example 'e' is 0). The rest are represented by two digits as we have seen before (so 'y' is 24). The digits 2 and 1 cannot be used individually as this would confuse the decoder as they are the vertical axis numbers as well as being in the horizontal axis. The columns and rows can be numbered differently in any agreed way in other messages. The '/' symbol indicates a shift from words to numbers or back.

So the (quite true) plaintext, 'Used in 1937 by Spanish Communists', would be enciphered as:

u	s	e	d	i	n	1	9	3	7	b	y	s	p	a
28	4	0	18	5	6	211	9	3	721	10	24	4	20	8

n	i	s	h	c	o	m	m	u	n	i	s	t	s
6	5	4	15	19	7	11	11	28	6	5	4	9	4

In five-digit blocks (plus a final block of two), with each plaintext number digit repeated in case of transmission errors, it now appears as:

28401 85621 11993 37721 10244 20865 41519 71111
28654 94

The message could be sent as it is, or transposed back into letters using the bifid cipher method.

XXDFD AXGDF FDGAX
FXXXD

5 Code wars

Communication via telegraph and radio could be intercepted, so encryption was an important tool in both world wars and the diplomatic messages that led to them. Therefore code breaking reached new heights of significance and expertise in the first half of the 20th century. In both wars, the losers wrongly believed they had impregnable, secure code systems. Cryptanalysts sought ever-speedier ways of decrypting pioneered advances, which led to the modern computer.

Field codes and ciphers

The military have long been the force that pushes for improved cryptography, and phrases such as trench code and field cipher indicate how codes were used in action, requiring simple, fast systems that relied on memory rather than a manual.

Code or cipher?

One of the first actions the British took in World War I was to cut the cables laid across the North Sea by the Germans. This forced their enemy to send signals on cables controlled by the Allies, or by radio, both of which allowed them to be intercepted. The move reveals the importance of encrypting and decrypting communication in wartime. The debate about whether to opt for codes or ciphers for secret communication was particularly heated during World War I. Each had its merits and drawbacks (see the tables below and opposite).

For these reasons, navies more than armies liked codes, because a ship offers relatively good security for storing code books, which were bound in metal so that they could be thrown overboard and would sink before they could be captured. An army on the move could not ensure security to this degree, but

Codes

Advantages	Disadvantages
▶ High level of confidentiality if code books are secure.	▶ Large code books are difficult to transport safely and securely.
▶ Allows use of a wide vocabulary.	▶ Can be attacked bit by bit as each code word reveals its secret.
▶ Long phrases used regularly can be communicated concisely with one word or number.	▶ If your enemy captures a code book without your knowledge, they can read all your messages as fast as you.
	▶ Capture of the code book requires the creation of a new one.

Ciphers

Advantages	Disadvantages
▶ No bulky code book to transport. ▶ Can be adjusted regularly, for example by changing keywords, to maintain security.	▶ Can take longer to decipher, slowing down communication. ▶ Transmission errors possible, very hard to spot and cause confusion in deciphering. ▶ Messages sometimes have to be sent twice – gold dust to opposing cryptanalysts. ▶ Operators of the system get lazy and take short cuts, which offer clues to the enemy.

they believed codes were harder to break than ciphers. Both sides began to use trench codes to encode communication by telephone. It created an enormous administrative task: for example, the German trench codes eventually comprised 4,000 code words, which were changed every fortnight.

Such was the speed of change at times on the battlefields of World War I that occasionally armies would send orders in plaintext, to be acted on instantly, knowing that the enemy would still not be able to react, even though they could read the opposition's instruction. This was backed by the reassuring knowledge that while the enemy could intercept and understand this message, it gave them no clue as to how to solve other secret communications, whereas every coded message provided more data for cryptanalysts to study.

Field ciphers

Field ciphers are ciphers requiring little equipment such as conversion tables or apparatus, being reliant on an easily remembered and changed keyword. They are ideally suited to communication by an

must know

Open to attck
Sending unencrypted messages carries a risk. In August 1914, the Russians were forced to communicate in plaintext because their cryptosystem had reached only parts of their army. The Germans read the messages and, as a result, switched their point of attack in the Battle of Tannenberg, the heaviest Russian defeat of the whole war. This was one of several military disasters that was blamed on open communications being intercepted.

must know

Why five?
The letters chosen
for the ABFGX
cipher were the
ones least like each
other in Morse
code, making
mistakes less likely
in transmission
and decrypting.

army on a fast-moving battlefield. The ideal field cipher is one
that is easily operated by one person who carries the system
mostly in their head.

The most famous field cipher was used by German forces
during World War I, and is called the ABFGX cipher, a cunning
blend of substitution and transposition that created messages
using only five letters. The method required a mixed alphabet
grid and a keyword, both of which were changed daily.

First, a mixed alphabet was created, with 'i' and 'j'
combined:

	A	D	F	G	X
A	k	r	z	v	l
D	f	t	s	x	i/j
F	g	m	o	h	w
G	b	e	q	p	c
X	d	a	y	n	u

The plaintext, here 'Just five letters', was fractionated:

j	u	s	t	f	i	v	e	l	e	t	t	e	r	s
DX	XX	DF	DD	DA	DX	AG	GD	AX	GD	DD	DD	GD	AD	DF

Then the resultant monoalphabetic substitution ciphertext was
written in columns under the keyword 'ZEBRA':

Z	E	B	R	A
D	X	X	X	D
F	D	D	D	A
D	X	A	G	G
D	A	X	G	D
D	D	D	D	G
D	A	D	D	F

Finally, the transposed message was read in columns, following the alphabetical order of the letters in the keyword (A= 1, B = 2, E = 3, R=4, Z = 5): DAGDGF XDAXDD XDXADA XDGGDD DFDDDD. It would be transmitted in batches of five letters:

DAGDG FXDAX DDXDX ADAXD GGDDD FDDDD

This cipher evolved into the ADFGVX cipher, which created a 36-strong alphabet, allowing the introduction of numbers. A major benefit for its users was that enciphering only required two simple steps, and only six (and earlier, five) letters were used in transmission, so it could be sent rapidly. The Allied forces made huge efforts to solve it and it was broken by French army Lieutenant Georges Painvin. His solution began with finding two messages that started or finished in the same way. This is called a 'crib'. From this, the Allies were able to decipher first the ciphertext as it would be prior to transposition and then use frequency analysis on the ciphertext. On quiet, low traffic days, they were less likely to find a pair of messages with identical beginnings or endings.

Cribs

We are all creatures of habit, and so are many organizations with their agreed practices and procedures. As a result, even encrypted communication can follow patterns and become predictable. Once this occurs, the code breaker has a crib: a word or a piece of text that they already know is repeated somewhere in an encrypted message. This is extremely valuable as the code breaker can then search for patterns that relate to it, rather than just fishing for clues. Genuine examples of cribs from one or other of the world wars include:

▶ Stereotyped messages such as 'Nothing to report'.
▶ Weather reports that were sent at the same time each day and in the same format.

must know

Creating cribs
One way to create a crib for the Allies was to bomb a certain spot, wait for the Germans to report it, and use the map grid reference of the bombed location as a crib.

▶ Messages beginning, 'It is my honour to inform your Excellency'.

▶ Sending well-known proverbs as test messages.

▶ Using patriotic words such as 'Kaiser' or 'Deutschland' as keywords.

Gardening for cribs

Such is the value of cribs that code breakers took actions to try to prompt messages with certain words that then become a crib, a practice known as 'gardening'. For example:

▶ In World War I, the Allies bombarded certain trenches knowing it would make the Germans send messages about those parts of the battlefield.

▶ In World War II, the Americans sent an uncoded message that a ship needed fresh water, knowing the Japanese would intercept and report it, thus revealing their code name for the ship.

Making the most of mistakes

Lazy operators not changing their keywords or their style of transmission is another habit that leaves the doors open for code breakers. Even better, operators who make mistakes are invaluable because they are often asked to repeat the message. If they do this with a new cipher or keyword, the code breaker can create a crib by decrypting the first transmission. Another mistake is chattiness. During World War II, staff on the German U-boats were understandably lonely and were encouraged to communicate with each other and with land, believing that their powerful codes were unbreakable. However, Allied cryptanalysts found there were messages about birthdays, toothaches and friends. The more messages sent, the more clues they gained about the ciphers being used.

The ultimate crib

The ultimate crib is, of course, the code book itself. During World War II, the capture of a German submarine gave the Allies access to the German code bible, the book of daily settings for the Enigma coding machine (see page 120-7). Assuming this document had sunk to the depths, the Germans did not change their ciphers, and the Allies were able to listen in to U-boat communication.

The Zimmerman telegram

In 1917, a decrypted telegram led the US to enter World War I. Named after its sender, German Foreign Minister Arthur Zimmerman, it offered Mexico American territory in return for joining the war. Intercepted by the British, it led US President Woodrow Wilson to join the Allies in fighting Germany and her partners. The British were able to decipher much of the message because it had been partly encrypted using codes with which they were already familiar: they had a crib.

The machine age

After centuries of using pencil and paper methods for encryption and decryption, the impact of cryptography on World War I encouraged governments and the military to create stronger codes and ciphers. Inventions such as the telegraph, calculator, typewriter and cash register, highlighted the new role of technology, and the push was on to invent automated cipher machines.

The Jefferson wheel

In fact, the first encrypting machine had been invented, and largely forgotten, in the 1790s by Thomas Jefferson, an incredibly gifted man who was to become the third president of the US. The machine is a simple device: a set of between 20 and 40 discs, or wheels, each with the alphabet written on them in random order. The discs are mounted in a row to form a cylinder. Jefferson was aware that the more wheels there were, the better, and suggested having 36, which gave a huge number of possible settings (nearly 372 followed by 39 zeros!, calculated from 1 x 2 x 3 x ... x 35 x 36).

To operate the Jefferson wheel, you would create your message in plaintext along one row, reading across the discs, then copy out any other row of letters, which would be gibberish. The recipient simply re-creates the line of nonsense, then scans the other rows until he finds a readable message. The cipher could be changed by removing the discs and replacing them in a different agreed order. It was a brilliant invention, years ahead of its time, yet Jefferson seems to have forgotten about it. In his defence, he was a busy chap: at various times he was a statesman, diplomat, writer, lawyer, main author of the 1776 American Declaration of Independence, founder of the University of Virginia, architect, agriculturalist, horticulturalist, archaeologist ... so perhaps he can be excused for forgetting that he had invented the best, most easily operated polyalphabetic enciphering system so far in history, which at the time was just about unbreakable.

Re-inventing the wheel

From 1922 to 1943 the US Army sent ciphered messages using a cylindrical device made up of lettered aluminium wheels, and known as M-94. It was almost the same as the Jefferson wheel, and had been developed by two officers in 1917. They had been inspired in turn by the Bazières cylinder, an 1891 re-invention of Jefferson's cipher device.

---

must know

Ending a 200-year mystery
The Bazières cylinder is named after Etienne Bazières, who earned a place in code-breaking history by breaking the famous Great Cipher. This was a 17th-century creation by father and son team Antione and Bonaventure Rossignol, who worked for French kings Louis XIII and XIV. Their complex cipher substituted certain syllables and employed tricks such as codes instructing 'ignore the previous group'. The code of choice for the French monarchy, it confounded cryptanalysts for 200 years until Bazières cracked it with painstaking work combined with some inspired guessing of the phrases used as keys.

Enigma

The breaking of the Enigma cipher was one of the great achievements of World War II, and in the history of cryptography. Some historians believe that it shortened the war by a year and saved millions of lives.

Making Enigma

The saga begins with a massive irony. In 1923, publication of Winston Churchill's book about World War I, *The World Crisis*, together with the Royal Navy's history of that war, revealed how the Allies had cracked German ciphers and listened in on their communications. This was a monumental shock to the German military, who had never considered that their codes had been broken. They realized a massive upgrade in their encryption systems was required. So the tip-off that led to them using Enigma came from the future leader of Britain, who later stood between them and victory in World War II.

There is a further irony at this point. The Enigma machine inventor, Arthur Scherbius, failed to sell it to the German military and made it available on the commercial market, bringing it to the attention of the rest of the world. By the time the Nazi war machine started using Enigma, various other powers had gained some knowledge of how it worked. This information was crucial in the later breaking of the Enigma codes. Bizarrely, history repeated itself because the Germans considered their 30,000 Enigma machines formed an unbreakable system and, for the second time, did not know that the Allies were listening in on their communication for much of the war.

The Enigma machine

The Enigma machine was by far the most complicated enciphering system created at the time. It looked like a typewriter with parts stuck on the sides, which had been put in a wooden box. There were many different versions, commercial and military, and its workings were improved several times during the war.

In essence, Enigma was a set of rotating wheels wired in several ways so that a message whose letters had already been substituted was repeatedly scrambled to create a monumental number of variations that defied any known analysis because it left no glimmer of a pattern. Depending on the version of the machine used, Enigma made between nine and eleven changes to every letter of the plaintext on its route to the ciphertext.

Its main letter-scrambling device was a set of three electromagnetic wheels called rotors, each marked with an alphabet, similar to the concept of the Jefferson wheel (see page 118). With single-notched rotors, the 'period' of the machine (the possible number of shifts before returning to the original setting) was 17,576 (26 x 26 x 26), helping to protect against overlapping alphabets. This, in itself, is a relatively simple substitution cipher, vulnerable to frequency analysis. However:

▶ Each time a key was struck, the first rotor changed position, altering the substituting pattern so that each letter was encrypted with a new encrypting alphabet.

▶ The rotors were connected so that when the first rotor had shifted 26 times, the next rotor then advanced one place. With three rotors this meant

must know

Rotor race
Many inventors were working on the concept of a rotor machine in the early 20th century. The first to make one were a pair of Dutch naval officers, Theo van Hengel and R. P. C. Spengler.

that the machine only returned to its original setting after 676 letters had been typed in.

▶ The rotors could be re-ordered (so instead of 123 they could be in 132, 213, 231, 312 or 321 order). This allowed six more permutations, vastly increasing the number of alphabet combinations (6 x 17,576 = 105,456).

▶ Further internal wiring linked the rotors to a plugboard, which exchanged up to six letters, for example swapping around D and F, to make encryption even more complex.

▶ The third rotor was connected to a non-rotating rubber device (confusingly called a reflector), which connected back to the third rotor.

The extra wiring and the reflector also made the machine 'reciprocal': this means it was able to both encipher and decipher messages – a huge convenience. Enigma was also relatively simple to set up and operate, requiring only a key that detailed the rotors to be used, the rotor order and starting positions and the plugboard connections. Every day a new key was taken from a code book that contained 28 new settings, and which was issued every four weeks. A captured Enigma machine was useless without this code book.

Enigmatically impregnable
Scherbius calculated that it would take 1,000 cryptanalysts testing four keys a minute, for 24 hours a day, a total of 1.8 billion years to find every one, and this was with an early version of Enigma before extra variations were introduced. A modern computer testing for a million different keys per second would

take nearly 227,000 years to check them all. Since the machine also defied frequency analysis and pattern analysis, it is quite understandable that its cipher was considered unbreakable.

Breaking Enigma

Enigma was broken by a mixture of subterfuge, brilliant mathematics and bad habits on the part of its operators. The story begins in Poland shortly after the Germans began using the machine.

In 1929, an Enigma machine sent by the Germans from Berlin to Warsaw was mistakenly not put in a sealed diplomatic bag, allowing the package to be intercepted without fear of a diplomatic incident. The Poles were able to study the wiring of the machine and gain some understanding of its workings.

Two years later, an impoverished and resentful German working at Enigma's command centre, Hans-Thilo Schmidt, sold information about the wiring of the machine and layout of code books to the French secret service. They couldn't understand it and passed it on to the Poles.

The Polish Cipher Bureau was particularly keen to decipher the communications of their neighbour and had a team investigating Enigma. In 1932, cryptanalyst Marian Rejewski noticed patterns in the way operators indicated new settings for each message by sending an identical twice-encrypted, three-letter message. In a year of number crunching, Rejewski brilliantly discerned a pattern in the scrambled letters, which considerably lessened the decryption task.

must know

Watery secrets
With the German naval version of Enigma the hardest to break, submarines were attacked in the hope of retrieving their code books. The Allies would board the captured U-boat, remove the invaluable documents, then sink the craft to fool the Germans into thinking the documents were safe on the seabed.

Rejewski and his colleagues were able to make six machines that copied Enigma's encryption technique – one for each of the rotor orders. These machines could find the day key in a matter of hours. The ticking sound they made as they tested every possibility looking for a match earned them the nickname 'bombes'.

Secret secrets

The head of the Polish Cipher Bureau, Major Gwido Langer, followed the cunning management strategy of not informing his staff that, in fact, Schmidt was still selling information and that he already had the answers that they were spending days deducing. He did this in anticipation that when their pet spy was no longer supplying information, his department would still be able to read secret German messages.

However, from 1938 the German military increased the number of rotors from three to five, and later the number of plugboard cables from six to ten, raising the possible number of keys to 159,000,000,000,000,000,000. Although they knew how to break the strengthened code, the Polish cryptanalysts simply did not have the enormous resources required to do it. When Schmidt stopped selling the code books shortly after, Enigma was again impenetrable. However, the Polish Cipher Bureau was years ahead of other cryptanalysts in its working knowledge of Enigma and how to break it, and when they shared their expertise with the Allies in 1939 (just weeks before Poland was invaded), it kick-started a new impetus to crack Enigma.

Bletchley Park

British code breaking during World War II was based at the Government Code and Cipher School at Bletchley Park, an estate in the middle of England within easy reach of London and handily located near a railway line linking the universities of Oxford and Cambridge. Bletchley Park sprouted several large sheds to accommodate its offices and staff, who were all forbidden from revealing the nature of their work, even to their families. Each day, the staff would collect the intercepted Morse code German messages and begin work on breaking the ciphers, which had been changed at midnight. They used a blend of equipment, knowledge of German procedures, mathematical analysis and instinct to guide their endeavours. It generally took about two hours to break that day's codes and the intelligence revealed through the war (code named Ultra) saved thousands of Allied lives and changed its course.

Chinks in the Enigma armour

There were a number of characteristics of Enigma and the way it was operated that reduced the number of possibilities requiring investigation each day:

▶ No letter could be encrypted as itself, so a ciphertext A was never a plaintext 'a'.

▶ Letters could not be encrypted as their neighbours in the alphabet, so 'b' could never be A or C.

▶ Enigma was reciprocal, so if 'f' was enciphered as K, then 'k' would be transformed into F.

▶ The rotors were not allowed to be in the same place two days running. So if the order one day was

Sum help
British cryptanalysts had traditionally been an 'old boy' and 'old girl' network of linguists and classicists chosen for their ability to solve crosswords. Polish number-crunching breakthroughs encouraged the addition of mathematicians to the new code-breaking team based at Bletchley Park.

123, it could not be 213 the next day because the third rotor hadn't moved.

▶ There was a pattern in how the rotor wheels turned.

While all these were valuable in reducing the number of possibilities requiring investigation, the crucial attack weapon was a crib – some part of the plaintext that was already known or guessable. For example, weather reports were sent in at the same time, in the same format, each day, so decrypters learned to guess where words such as 'weather' were likely to be, giving them a massive head start. The Poles had used cribs in their early cryptanalysis of Enigma codes, locating the German word for 'to' followed by a space indicator: 'AnX'.

Finally, and some argue most importantly, a powerful weapon for the decrypter was quite simply operator error:

▶ In choosing the settings, cipher operators develop habits, such as choosing letters from the same row of the keyboard, or a girlfriend's initials, when selecting the message key. Code breakers learnt to recognize these and to try popular options first.

▶ Any mistake by German communications staff helped the code breakers: the necessity to re-send a message created a valuable crib allowing comparison of two ciphertexts, or a procedural flaw (for example, a sloppy operator sending a second message using the same key settings) weakened the security of the encryption.

Turing

The most famous of the cryptographers working at Bletchley Park was Alan Turing. A brilliant mathematician, in 1937 he published a paper describing a hypothetical device that uses algorithms to answer any question that has a logical solution. Now known as a Turing machine, it closely resembles the modern programmable computer.

Turing was taken on as a cryptanalyst at Bletchley Park and designed a machine for breaking the Enigma codes. It took the Polish 'bombe' method (after which it was nicknamed) a stage further by electronically testing a crib against a selection of possible keys until it found the plaintext. Once the machine was refined, with the help of a good crib it could break that day's code in two hours. This was tremendously valuable for military intelligence.

Other World War II code breaking

The Germans and Japanese, wrongly confident of the security of their communications, unwittingly provided much invaluable data to their enemies, which undoubtedly changed the course of the war. The British and American governments recognized the value of secret intelligence and poured money into cryptanalysis. However, a common theme in the breaking of the three powerful codes described here is that, had operators not made mistakes, these codes would have stayed secure for far longer.

From fish to computers

Hitler's communication with his most senior generals went via the Lorenz SZ-40 telecipher, a more complex version of the Enigma that used digital code – turning the message into binary data (see page 134).

Staff at Bletchley Park christened the new-style messages FISH, and the machine that created them TUNNY. They broke the code through a stroke of luck. On 30 August 1941, a German operator sent a message of about 4,000 characters. There were problems receiving it, so he was asked to re-transmit, at which point, probably in a frantic hurry, he made what turned out to be two (cryptographically) fatal errors:

▶ He didn't change the starting settings of his teletypewriter.
▶ He used abbreviations and short cuts, removing about 500 characters.

By comparing the two messages, the British cryptanalysts, led by John Tiltman, were able to create a crib. Now they could decipher FISH messages, but it took up to six weeks, by which time most of the intelligence was out of date. The solution to this was to build a machine capable of mechanical analysis of data, but also able to adapt as the problem changed. It was called Colossus and it was the first programmable computer. It speeded up the decryption of Hitler's messages significantly, and the intelligence revealed the success of the Allied plan to deceive Germany about where the 1944 invasion of France would take place. Colossus would have made an equally important contribution to the development of computers if it had not been kept a secret for another thirty years.

Purple code

The American achievement in breaking the Japanese PURPLE cipher certainly contributed to the outcome of the war in the Pacific. The American code breakers, known as the SIS (Signals Intelligence Service), broke a Japanese code in the 1930s, dubbing it RED in communication to avoid revealing that it was broken. This strategy failed, however, and Japan's far more complicated successor, introduced in 1939, was known in the US as PURPLE.

Japanese is a complex language with more than 20,000 written symbols in all, which are then written in different styles according to how they are pronounced. Since this was too complicated to encipher, the Japanese instead opted to write Japanese sounds phonetically using a Roman alphabet, which they called 'Romanji'.

The plaintext was fed into a machine that encrypted in a similar pattern to Enigma, except instead of rotors it used switches like that of a telephone exchange, combined with an extremely complicated wiring system. As with the Germans and Enigma, the Japanese believed it to be impregnable.

Breaking the purple cipher

The SIS broke the PURPLE cipher mainly thanks to a brilliant cryptanalyst called William Friedman. He got hold of a tabulating machine that used punched cards to monitor accounts information and used it to analyze Japanese communication. PURPLE was broken by:

▶ Statistical analysis using the tabulating machine.

▶ Friedman and his staff working out how the Japanese were choosing the message keys.

▶ Some of the same messages being sent in both ciphers during the transition from RED to PURPLE, providing a crib.

▶ The Japanese sending messages in a uniform format with predictable beginnings and endings.

▶ In 1940, the amount of communications traffic between Japan and its embassies increasing hugely because of negotiations with the Nazis, providing a large flow of encrypted data to analyze.

Even though they had never seen one, Friedman and his staff manufactured their own version of the PURPLE encoding machine so that they could understand how it encrypted. In the end they were using it to decrypt messages as fast as the Japanese.

JN-25

PURPLE code was used for diplomatic communication. Japanese naval messages, however, were sent in a completely unrelated (genuine) code, dubbed JN-25 because it was the 25th-known system used by the Japanese navy. Only a navy could use such a code, because it comprised more than 30,000 phrases, words and letters, each given a five-digit number – securely storable on a ship, but not by a mobile army. The bulky encrypting and decrypting code books were changed every few months.

A weakness in large-scale code systems is that since dictionaries are alphabetical, the numerical codes can provide clues to the starting letter. For example, if 'Attack' has the number 200, it is likely that lower numbers will be for words appearing before that word in a dictionary and vice versa. The JN-25 code counteracted this by altering the numbers with a complicated addition system.

Again, the code was solved partly because of blunders by its operators, who continued to use outdated codes that had been broken by staff at Bletchley Park, who had discerned a recognizable pattern in the numbers being based on multiples of three. Reading JN-25 code messages gave the US a major advantage in the Battle of Midway on 5 June 1942. The American victory in this battle marked a turning point in the war in the Pacific.

1000011 1001111 1000100
1000101 1010011 1001001
1001110 1000011 1011001
1000010 1000101 1010010
1010011 1010000 1000001
1000011 1000101

6 Codes in cyberspace

Until the 1970s, cryptography was only used by a few hobbyists and for military and diplomatic communication. Its public use had been restricted to a few periods when it had value, for example, romantic messages sent via Victorian newspapers, and cost-saving short cuts using telegrams. The computer age has changed all that. The introduction of computers followed by the development of email and the internet has created a new need for large-scale cryptography.

Computer encryption

The binary number system was first used as a coding method in the 19th century. It became the computer language of the 21st century. Therefore today's plethora of electronic encryption systems are based on the simple idea that '1' stands for 'on' and '0' means 'off'.

On and off

Computer language is binary code. This is a number system with a base of two, so the only digits used are 0 and 1. In our base-ten decimal number system, '1234' is one thousand, two hundreds, three tens and four units. In base two, the first seven columns have the following values:

64	32	16	8	4	2	1

So '2' is expressed as 10, '3' as 11, '4' as 100, '5' as 101 and '6' as 110. Each digit in binary code is known as a 'bit', and each 'bit' is either 'on' or 'off', with a value of 'true' or 'false'.

In 1874, Emile Baudot patented a five-bit code, which allowed representation of characters, some punctuation and numbers using binary code. This was intended for use in the pulsing 'on', 'off' telegraphic communication system, and replaced Morse code in the mid 20th century. Baudot's code had 32 five-digit 'words' allowing it to represent every character in the alphabet plus some other symbols, but special signals doubled its capacity by

Bilateral cipher

In 1563, Francis Bacon published his bilateral cipher in which all letters are represented by 'a' and 'b'. It bears an uncanny resemblance to five-bit binary code (see opposite). The Baconian alphabet is:

A =	aaaaa	N =	abbaa
B =	aaaab	O =	abbab
C =	aaaba	P =	abbba
D =	aaabb	Q =	abbbb
E =	aabaa	R =	baaaa
F =	aabab	S =	baaab
G =	aabba	T =	baaba
H =	aabbb	UV =	baabb
IJ =	abaaa	W =	babaa
K =	abaab	X =	babab
L =	ababa	Y =	babba
M =	ababb	Z =	babbb

So 'Bacon' is enciphered as aaaabaaaaaaaabaabbababbaa.

indicating if the subsequent 'words' represented letters (11111, also expressed as +++++) or numbers (11011, also expressed as ++−++).

Baudot's code developed into the seven-bit American Standard Code for Information Interchange (ASCII) code that continues to be used by computers today.

Capital letters are represented by ASCII binary numbers (see chart on page 136). Numbers are expressed as 1 = 0110001, 2 = 0110010, 3 = 0110011 and so on.

This, of course, creates a simple code. The message 'Binary' is written as:

1000010 1001001 1001110 1000001 1010010 1011001

which can also be written as a single string or broken into blocks of five. The following are four kinds of computer encryption that can still be done (at an infinitely slower pace than a computer!) by hand, and so could still be used as a simple cipher.

ASCII binary numbers			
A	1000001	S	1010011
B	1000010	T	1010100
C	1000011	U	1010101
D	1000100	V	1010110
E	1000101	W	1010111
F	1000110	X	1011000
G	1000111	Y	1011001
H	1001000	Z	1011010
I	1001001	1	0110001
J	1001010	2	0110010
K	1001011	3	0110011
L	1001100	4	0110100
M	1001101	5	0110101
N	1001110	6	0110110
O	1001111	7	0110111
P	1010000	8	0111000
Q	1010001	9	0111001
R	1010010		

Stream cipher

In a binary code, changing every bit would be very easy to decipher, but creating a repeating string of bits out of a keyword (known as a key stream sequence) means that '0' can be interpreted as 'leave' and '1' as 'change'. This concept was introduced in 1919 by Gilbert Vernam as a way of enciphering Baudot messages. It is best expressed in a simple table and is known as the XOR operation:

must know

Still used
Vernam's cipher is the basis for the RC4 encryption method still used to protect internet traffic and wireless networks today (although it is being superseded).

		Plaintext		
		1	0	
Key	1	0	1	**Ciphertext**
	0	1	0	

Binary code can be transmitted in 'on' or 'off' pulses where a timing mechanism checks the line, say, every tenth of a second, to see if a pulse can be sensed or not. Binary code can also be transferred to paper tape by punching, or not punching, holes at regular intervals.

Vernam devised a system in which two punched tapes, one holding the plaintext, the other a key of random numbers, were fed together into an adapted teletypewriter. If two holes matched up, a hole, or pulse was transmitted. If two holes did not match up, it left a space.

This allowed instant transmission of messages typed in plaintext, automatically encrypted, and automatically decrypted by a receiver using an identical key tape. This was a huge advance in

must know

The one-time pad
If the key to a Vernam cipher is utterly random and is used only once, this is known as a 'one-pad cipher', considered to be genuinely unbreakable, although there is much mathematical debate about whether a sequence can ever be truly random (see page 103).

cryptography, partly because no one had to sit and encrypt or decrypt the message, which was typed in as normal, transmitted in code, yet fed out at the other end as plaintext – you didn't need a skilled cryptanalyst at either end of the process (although you needed someone who could run the machine properly).

Using Vernam's method, but using today's seven-bit ASCII language, the plaintext 'computers' can be encrypted using the keyword BAUDOT as follows (the keyword is repeated as often as is needed):

Message	C	o	m	p	u	t	e	r	s
ASCII message	1000011100111110011011010000101010110101001000101101001010011								
Keyword in ASCII	1000010100000110101011000100100111110101001000010100001101010								
Ciphertext	0000001000111000110000010100001101000000000000111001001100001								

The ciphertext is created by adding the digits of the ASCII message and ASCII keyword, i.e. $1 + 1 = 0$; $1 + 0 = 1$; $0 + 1 = 1$. This is called a stream cipher. The message is decrypted by reversing this process.

Block cipher

Another encryption method is the block cipher in which the bits are grouped into threes, which can then be converted into digits, using the ASCII binary numbers (see page 136). For example, the same 'computers' message can now be encrypted as shown at the top of the opposite page.

Block	100	001	110	011	111	001	101	101	000	010	101
Number	4	1	6	3	7	1	5	5	0	2	5

Block	011	010	100	100	010	110	100	101	010	011
Number	3	2	4	4	2	6	4	5	2	3

This shorter ciphertext of 41637155025324426452 3
can still easily be converted back to binary numbers
and then into characters.

HEX

An alternative coding system is hexadecimal
notation (HEX), which gives values to blocks of four
bits as follows:

0000 = 0	0001 = 1	0010 = 2	0011 = 3
0100 = 4	0101 = 5	0110 = 6	0111 = 7
1000 = 8	1001 = 9	1010 = A	1011 = B
1100 = C	1101 = D	1110 = E	1111 = F

Using HEX, the 'Computers' plaintext is converted
like this:

ASCII	1000	0111	0011	1110	0110	1101	0000	1010
HEX	8	7	3	E	6	D	0	A

ASCII	1011	0101	0010	0010	1101	0010	1010	0011
HEX	B	5	2	2	D	2	A	3

Note that a null '0' has been placed at the front of
the final block in the ASCII text to maintain the block
size of four digits. The ciphertext is now:
873E6D0AB522D2A3.

Key distribution

With the coming of the internet and email electronic communications, messages are bounced off satellites around the globe. This is fast, but of course such signals can be picked up by anyone, so it is easy for someone with the right knowledge and software to intercept messages. Stream and block ciphers are efficient methods of encryption but suffer the problem of every key-based encryption method: distributing the key.

---

must know

Alice and Bob
For some reason, most explanations about message verification and the use of keys use the names Alice and Bob – involving both sexes and offering human-sounding substitutes for A and B. The evil interceptor is usually referred to as Eve, which is either a Biblical reference or short for 'eavesdropper'.

Big issues

In the 1983 film *Superman III*, Richard Pryor plays Gus Gorman, who changes the computer payroll program so that it pays him all the fractions of cents unpaid in other employees' salaries, making him a fortune. This concept of stealing fractions of pennies a slice at a time is called a 'salami attack'. There are plenty of stories of employees who interfere with computer programs for financial gain or retribution against their bosses. While many of these may be urban myths, there is no doubt that the phenomenon of hackers breaking into computer systems and stealing or amending data or programs has become one of the biggest issues facing this technology.

The key ideas here are:

▶ Authentication: how do you know an email comes from where it says it did?

▶ Signature verification: how do you know that the person who has apparently sent the message really did so?

The solution is for both parties to communicate using an agreed encryption system.

Public key enciphering

Academics and mathematicians struggled to find a way to keep coded communication secure for decades. There is a simple theory of how to achieve message security:

Alice wants to send a secret message to Bob.

▶ She puts it in a box, padlocks it and sends it to Bob without the key.

▶ Bob attaches his own padlock to the box and returns it, again without the key.

▶ Alice now removes her padlock and returns the box.

▶ Bob can now open the box with his own key.

This is known as an asymmetric key system, in which a different key (or, if you prefer, combination) is required to decrypt rather than encrypt. In a symmetric key system, Bob would simply use a copy of Alice's key to open the box – re-introducing the key distribution problem. The asymmetric system is fine if physical keys are used, because two different keys can (separately) lock one box. However, if the key is a code, the process won't work because Bob has to put Alice's box inside another box, which he then locks and dispatches. Now she can't get inside to her original box.

Private keys

Here is a slightly different process, this time using numbers:

▶ Alice and Bob both select a secret number each. She chooses 12, he goes for 37. These are their private keys.

▶ They agree a third, shared number, 23.

▶ Alice adds her secret number and the shared number: $12 + 23 = 35$.

Prime numbers

Prime numbers have no factors apart from 1 and themselves. So 3, 5 and 7 are prime, but 2, 4, 6 and 9 are not as they can be divided by other numbers. The prime numbers used in public key encryption usually have five or more digits.

▶ Bob also adds his secret number and their shared number: 37+ 23 = 60.

▶ They swap the answers they got, then add their own original secret number. So Alice's sum is 60 + 12, and Bob's is 35 + 37.

Both answers are 72, the message key, but they haven't revealed their secret number to each other. Of course, the drawback with this is that addition is reversible, so if an eavesdropper (traditionally known as Eve) overhears, say, Alice's sending the value of 35 and subtracts their public shared number, 23, she identifies Alice's private key of 12, allowing her to decrypt the message.

However, not every calculation is reversible in this way. In modular arithmetic, numbers change after they reach a certain value. The clearest simple example is a clock face. Add on six hours from 9 o'clock and you reach 15 o'clock, known as 3 o'clock. Similarly, count back five hours four times (5 x 4) from 12 o'clock and you reach 8 o'clock, not twenty. Another way of putting it is that if you were dividing using modular arithmetic, only the remainder would be shown as an answer (so 5 divided by 2 is 1, which is written as 5 mod 2 = 1). So modular arithmetic can create 'one-way functions' that are not easily reversed – just as when you make a glass of squash you can't separate the syrupy concentrate from the water you added.

In 1976, Martin Hellman hit upon a way of using modular arithmetic to allow Alice and Bob to exchange information in a similar way to the example above, using the results of their calculations as their key, knowing that no one listening in could find the key. The method is called the Diffie-Hellman-Merkle key exchange scheme after Hellman and his two colleagues. However, it needed to be made more efficient, with less exchanges of information, to be usable. This was achieved by the RSA and ElGamal systems, which employ the Diffie-Hellman-Merkle method with multi-digit prime numbers. Detailed explanations of the maths involved in the scheme can be found at these websites: http://en.wikipedia.org/wiki/Diffie-Hellman and www.vectorsite.net/ttcode_10.html

The RSA system

The maths hereon is incredibly complicated (see pages 186–8 for websites and books on it) but the basic idea is this:

Alice selects two very large prime numbers. She multiplies them to create an even bigger number of at least 100 digits. This huge number is open for all to see and is her public key. Anyone who wishes to send Alice an encrypted message does so using this number. Now only Alice can decrypt it, using her private key created via various modular calculations of her prime numbers. Anyone else trying to find her two original prime numbers would have to search for many years to find the correct two factors even if they were equipped with the fastest computers in the world. Alice can also reply to her correspondents encrypting her message in a way that they can decrypt.

RSA in action

Enciphering with RSA takes up a lot of computer power and time, so it is not suitable for enciphering

long messages. Instead, it is commonly used to
encipher a key for a block cipher, rather than the
actual message, which is encrypted with the block
cipher. This is known as 'hybrid encryption'.

Pretty Good Privacy

Computer encryption became a genuinely public
tool in the early 1990s with the advent of Pretty
Good Privacy (PGP), a computer program that
provides cryptographic privacy and authentication,
allowing anybody to use the RSA method of
encryption without having to deal with its complex
mathematics. It was invented by Phil Zimmerman
and is mainly used to protect email
communications, which otherwise are completely
unencrypted, although it can also be used to encrypt
other computer data.

Its introduction was stimulated by the
extraordinary rise in internet and email
communication, echoing the impact of the
invention of the telegram and radio systems in the
past. Communication has never been easier, and nor
has interference in it. Digital communication raises
a number of issues, stemming from the fact that
anyone, anywhere in the world, can send and
intercept messages. There are enormous
opportunities for fraud, scams and interference in
the workings of other computers.

In addition to the mountain of business and
personal communication, internet shopping has
become very big business. There is even speculation
that the money markets will one day have to include
an internet-only currency. Even without this, of
course, money is now transferred electronically,

which means it can be stolen from a keyboard, without having to resort to the risky business of bursting into a high-street branch wearing a balaclava and clutching a shotgun. As governments push for further labour-saving uses of digital communications, for example tax returns, the security of the information highway becomes even more important.

Most purchases made on the internet involve the use of cryptography to protect credit card numbers or other financial information. This is done via the Secure Sockets Layer (SSL) and, increasingly, Transport Layer Security (TLS). Pages protected by SSL have an 'https' prefix instead of the conventional 'http' one, and use a blend of protocols and algorithms to enable key exchange, authentication and communication in cipher.

Who keeps the keys?

An issue that keeps cropping up in modern cryptology is whether there should be a central bank of encryption keys, rather like a private telephone directory. Users would have to register with it and send messages through it. In theory, this will be very convenient as the need for encrypted communication increases. However, it adds to the number of links in the security chain, and if a hacker could break into that central bank of keys, they would have access to every message. Those suspicious of central government point out that this access to all communication may be the reason state officials want to have a central bank of keys in the first place. Fittingly given the history of cryptography, mistrust fuels the debate.

must know

Key point
Governments are concerned by the increasing use of encryption by criminals and terrorists. For example, the Aum Shinrykyo religious group, which released the nerve-gas on a Tokyo subway in 1995, encrypted their critical documents. Laws in Singapore and Malaysia force citizens who have encrypted files to hand over keys on demand, and the US, British and Indian governments have apparently considered similar laws. These will be unpopular with those who argue for the public's right to privacy.

Passwords and attacks

In the days when lovers communicated via coded newspaper advertisements, people had to make or find their own code systems. Nosy readers could amuse themselves by trying to break the codes with pencil and paper. Nowadays, the nearest most of us need to come to creative thinking when encrypting is making up a password. In contrast, the business of attacking codes is increasingly complex.

must know

A good password

So a good password should follow these rules:
▶ Use the maximum possible number of characters.
▶ Do not use recognized words or names.
▶ VaRy capiTallZation.
▶ Include random numbers or graphic signs as well as letters. This is known as 'salting'.

Passwords: the modern key

For most of us, thinking up a password or username to key into our computer is the nearest we get to having to create a secret code, and most people are terrible at it. Any system is only as strong as its weakest link, and passwords are by far the easiest form of encryption to attack.

There is a basic problem: we are encouraged to create passwords we can remember easily, and discouraged from writing them down. So there is a strong temptation to use words related to the task ('password' is a common password!) or names of family members, and to keep the password short – studies suggest more than one in seven passwords are only three keys long. Forcing people to change their password every month isn't effective because even if they follow the rule, they tend to choose passwords they have used already, often simply alternating them with each enforced change.

One of the biggest sins is to choose letter-only passwords, especially those that spell a word. But, of course, this is the easiest way to generate a username that you can be sure of remembering.

Someone who wants to find your password will try the most obvious choices first – family names, maiden name, mother's maiden name. In the age of the internet, such data is relatively easy to find. The computer can also be used to test out other possible passwords through a dictionary attack. In this, a computer simply tries every word in the dictionary until it hits the right one. Powerful machines can do this in a matter of seconds. If they fail, they'll do the same with reversed words, varied capitalization and extra numbers.

A more sophisticated way to find your password is a timing attack. This notes how long it takes you to key in your password, allowing the computer to calculate the likely number of characters in it. This system can also be used to measure how long it takes for a password to be rejected: the more time, the closer the guess is likely to be.

Another form of attack is 'password sniffing'. This is when a hacker installs software on your computer that stores the first few keystrokes of every session, which is very likely to include your password.

The trouble is, of course, that a good, complex password is then hard to remember, so you'll most probably need to write it down. Provided it is kept in a secure place (not on a note stuck to the computer) this is a sensible option – your attacker is probably tapping a keyboard thousands of miles away, not snooping around your desk. This method allows you to create trickier passwords without needing to make them memorable. You've got the same level of security as the code books that were used for centuries.

PINs

Encryption is used to protect financial information sent by hole-in-the-wall Automatic Teller Machines (ATMs). The customer places their plastic card with its magnetic strip (and, increasingly, its identifying 'chip') in the machine and enters their Personal Identification Number (PIN). This is communicated to a central computer, which checks the data and ascertains if the customer is permitted to make a withdrawal – so information has to pass both ways.

The four-digit PIN is 'padded' with extra digits and all data is sent in encrypted form using a Data Encryption Standard (DES) cipher. The PIN obviously takes the place of a 'password' or 'key', and since there are only 10,000 possible combinations of four digit numbers (a tiny figure compared to the multi-digit encryption possibilities generated by RSA) the ATM only allows three attempts to input the number before retaining the card. This is starting to seem generous given that a recently devised, extremely complex mathematical attack method can allegedly identify a PIN in about 15 guesses.

Forms of attack

Apparently one of the popular sayings at the NSA (the US National Security Agency, see page 155) is 'Attacks never get weaker'. In an age of global communications, they can also come from anywhere, at any time. This is in contrast to the past when attack depended first of all on stopping the messenger and then finding the slip of paper with the message on it. Today, once a message is sent, it stays out there in the system, vulnerable to the hacker for eternity.

There are many motives for attack, including malice, financial or commercial gain, a hacker setting themselves a challenge, and military benefit. Hackers attacked many US and NATO computer sites in the period of the break-up of Yugoslavia in the 1990s, for example. China and Taiwan allegedly engaged in an informal internet war in 1999.

The following is a description of various different forms of computer attack that can be made from anywhere in the world.

Brute force attacks

This is when a computer (or a set of them) simply tries every possible key to the message of a symmetric key cipher, or calculates the key factors used in an asymmetric cipher. Another example is a dictionary attack (see page 147) to identify a password by trying every known word.

The longer the key, the longer it will take for a brute force attack to succeed. At present, just identifying (not even checking) the values for a 128-bit key would take 100 years and need something like four nuclear reactors to power it. However, the technology improves by the day, and attacks are already measured in how many billion keys per second are tested (see also quantum cryptography, page 151).

Passive attacks

This is when the attacker listens in on communication without interacting with either party. An eavesdropper (it's Eve again) will 'tune in', trawling for passwords and other key information.

Active attacks

In an active attack, a hacker will add, delete or amend messages. They might, for example, re-route money to a different account, or plant a 'logic bomb' that can be triggered to become active in certain circumstances (if the employee is fired, for example).

Man in the middle attack

This is where the eavesdropper assumes the identity of another party (the Bob or the Alice), receiving, reading and then passing on messages to the right person. They can then simply listen in and collect data (this is called traffic analysis), or launch attacks such as denial of service, which bring down the whole system. Man in the middle attacks are also known as 'bucket brigade attacks' (because when there is a fire everyone stands in a line handing on the bucket).

Timing attack

This allows attacking of RSA keys by measuring how long cryptographic operations take, giving some insight into the length and nature of the key. A simple example is that a three-letter password takes up less time than a ten-character one. This is a form of 'side channel attack', which studies the actions of the computer under attack, rather than trying to replicate its calculations.

Of course there are ways to counter all of these forms of attack, mainly centred around checking authentication at all times. However, the history of cryptography shows that anything except a one-time pad code can eventually be broken, and, furthermore, the system is only as strong as its weakest link, which could be the hardware, the software, the networks or the people. After all, operator errors and slackness provided most of the clues that enabled Bletchley Park staff to break the Enigma codes. Basic security is another issue: gaining access to a machine when no one else is around is extremely effective, and is known as a 'lunchtime' or 'midnight' attack.

Quantum cryptography

Standard cryptography uses the laws of mathematics. Quantum cryptography uses the (highly complex) approaches of quantum mechanics and the physics of information. Communication is via photons in optical fibres or electrons in electric current. Since these are measurable and the channel is highly sensitive, any eavesdropping is immediately detected, so communication ceases until it can be kept safe.

Additionally, quantum computers are theoretically capable of incredibly fast factoring of large numbers, and so may be able to break RSA keys and crack DES and block ciphers far faster than the present generation of conventional computers.

To summarize: quantum technology may be able to find a way to crack codes faster than ever, but also to create secure, closed communications systems.

From black chambers to Cheltenham

The new doughnut-shaped spy centre in Cheltenham, the centre for signals intelligence in the UK, is the latest instalment in an international saga of concealing and probing communications that goes back for centuries.

Needling out information
One efficient method for seeing letters sealed in envelopes used a long needle rather like an old-fashioned sardine tin opening key. The needle was slipped into a corner of the envelope and turned, rolling up the paper inside. This could then be removed, copied and returned with the same method, leaving the envelope seal undisturbed. The only evidence of tampering was a small hole in the corner of the envelope.

Interception and deception

As explorers found new lands and places to trade with, countries needed diplomats to negotiate with other governments around the world. Inevitably, their messages would be intercepted, so they started using codes to conceal their content. Thus were the black chambers born. In many countries from the 16th century onwards, missives sent by foreign diplomats were routinely intercepted (often through bribing lowly-paid or greedy officials), opened, copied, re-sealed and sent on their way while clerks began breaking their codes. The practice became even more widespread when Britain separated from the Catholic church, as European countries and the papacy discussed the significance of the move and manoeuvred for political advantage from it.

This culture of secrecy and subterfuge stimulated cryptological endeavour. In 16th-century Venice, there were specialist schools on the subject, such was the demand for cryptography in this commercial and diplomatic centre. In England, the success of Elizabeth I's spymaster Walsingham in trapping her rival Mary (see page 81) was down to his efficient team of code breakers. In 1703, William Blencowe became the first Englishman to get a regular salary for cryptanalysis, receiving £100 a year and taking on the title Decrypter. Actually the job had been going for years, and Blencowe was taking over from his grandfather, John Wallis, who had trained him up in the dark art of unravelling secrets from coded writing.

At this time the most active and efficient black chamber in the world was the Geheime Kabinets-Kanzlei in Vienna, Austria. Here the day's intercepted missives arrived at 7 o' clock each morning, and were immediately dictated to secretaries to prepare the copy that the cryptanalysts would set to work decoding while the original message went on its way. Staff received financial incentives to master new languages and successful decryptions earned a substantial bonus, paid in person by the grateful King Karl V. They even got compensation for lost payment opportunities if one of their spy colleagues succeeded in stealing solutions direct from the embassies!

The analysts worked one week on, one week off in their Viennese office in recognition of the mental strain of their job. Indeed, there is a long history of rapid weight loss, stress and even nervous breakdown associated with the people working in this field. Cryptanalysts have often reported difficulty in sleeping, and recurrent dreams in which they are faced with impossibly big searches, like finding the right pebble on a beach.

Throughout the 18th and early 19th centuries, the black chambers were a secret mini industry that recruited the brightest minds and trained them to puzzle out the secret messages of friends and foes. Such was their expertise and value that they would often be kept on by new administrations and monarchs even when other officials who had served the previous government were disposed of.

Do they know what we know?

A recurring issue in the history of codebreaking is what to do with the information gathered, because of the risk that your opponent will realize their codes have been broken and so change them. Diplomats would remain tight-lipped as other ambassadors expressed opinions known to be the opposite of the view expressed in secret communication with their superiors. At one point, the Spanish government was a laughing stock among diplomats as its codes were so easy to break. They chuckled behind their hands, however, as the information they were receiving was so useful. In World War II, the British sometimes took no action over decrypted messages for fear of alerting the Germans to their ability to read Enigma messages, and at the time of the Pearl Harbor attack, the Americans knew the Japanese were going to break off diplomatic relations before their own ambassador could deliver the message.

An amusing variation on this theme of whether to reveal or conceal what you know is the story from Henry II's siege of Réalmont in 1628. A decoded intercepted message revealed the defenders had few supplies left. Henry sent in the decoded plaintext of their letter and they surrendered, knowing they had no chance of success.

Where are they now?

After World War I, the US founded MI-8, a code-breaking team under the guise of a New York commercial code production company. It was briefly closed down in 1931 on the orders of Secretary of State Henry Stimson, allegedly with the comment 'Gentlemen don't read other gentlemen's mail'. This deprived its key worker, Herbert Yardley, of an income so he wrote a book about his work, which alerted the Japanese to the fact that America had broken its codes, which were subsequently completely redeveloped.

Later reformed, MI-8 became the National Security Agency (NSA), combining its work with the Central Security Service (CSS).

Britain's black chamber moved to Room 40 at the Admiralty in London during World War I. It later evolved into Bletchley Park and various other sites, and today the Government Communications Headquarters (GCHQ) at Cheltenham is the UK centre for signals intelligence and information protection.

Both the American and British secrets-busting organizations run websites explaining some of what they do (see pages 186–8).

(see pages 186–8)

must know

Code courses
A number of universities in the UK and the US now offer courses about information security in which much of the content is about cryptography. Graduates tend to go on to work as IT security managers or consultants.

7 Codes in culture

Codes have found their way into books, films, art and music in many different ways. Sometimes they are recognizable as codes (especially as a plot device in fiction) and at others they lurk beneath the surface.

Books and films

Codes and ciphers are a useful plot device in stories because they intrigue the reader and allow the hero an opportunity to demonstrate their intelligence in solving the mystery. They were particularly popular in the 19th century when interest in cryptological matters reached new heights.

Codes in the Bible

A number of codes are said to be used in the Bible. They may have been included to add a sense of mystery, or to try to keep some Christian beliefs secret within the faith. Most common is the use of Atbash, a simple substitution cipher in which the alphabet is reversed (see page 74), which results in the word Shesbach replacing the place name Babel (also known as Babylon) in the original Hebrew.

Another is a substitution system called Albam, in which the 24-letter Hebrew alphabet is split into matching halves so that aleph becomes lamed, and beth becomes mem, creating the acronym for the process (a= l, b = m). The equivalent in English is 'a' becoming N, 'b' becoming O, etc. It is used in Isaiah 7:6, when 'Tabeel' replaces 'Remaliah'.

Numbers play an important part in the Bible, being used in place of words at times. For example Genesis 14:14 mentions that Abraham came to Lot with 318 servants, when 318 is the numerical value of the name of his servant, Eliezer. Numbers such as 666 (the number of the beast, cited in Revelation 13:18) and 888 (Jesus) are given great significance. The practice of converting words and sentences into numbers is called gematria.

Most controversially, Michael Drosnin's *The Bible Code* (1997) argued that the Good Book holds messages that are revealed through equidistant letter sequences (ELS). This is when you jump set distances between letters, which form phrases. Drosnin believed he had found various predictions of future events. This is extremely unlikely for the many reasons outlined below.

Some of the problems involved in discussing codes in the Bible are:

▶ It was not all written in the same language or at the same time.

▶ There are an estimated 33 different authors.

▶ There is not one agreed text, but many translations.

▶ Hebrew reads from right to left and has no vowels, which have to be introduced by the translator, so there is enormous scope for re-writing and re-interpretation.

▶ It is a huge 66 books and there are likely to be apparent ELS in any text as massive as this. After all, the King James Bible contains 791,328 words: it would be amazing if there were not some acronyms or ELS created purely by chance.

Shakespeare's secret

A great number of academics spend their careers picking apart the plays and poems of William Shakespeare in a bid to find out if he wrote them all, and if not, who did. Early last century some argued that the real author was statesman and writer Francis Bacon. Their evidence was based on:

▶ Reading messages from initial letters of words (steganography).

▶ Using a 21-letter alphabet like that of Elizabethan times, then replacing each letter with the one that comes four places later. Thus 'a' becomes E and so on. This shift reveals repeats of the name 'Bacon' in various spellings. However, it has been shown that carrying out this process on any text produces similar results: if you are looking for a hidden message you will surely find it somehow if the text is big enough.

The general consensus is that Shakespeare wrote his own works and did not use codes, ciphers or steganography.

A mysterious manuscript

In 1912, Polish-American book dealer Wilfrid M. Voynich, travelling in Italy, found a strange old illustrated book whose unidentified alphabet in an unintelligible language has defied expert analysis ever since. Known as the Voynich manuscript, the 240-page book has more than 170,000 characters, which seem to divide into about 35,000 words of various lengths. It is also illustrated with a bizarre collection of plants, herbal recipes, tiny naked people, astronomical charts and castles. The latter have helped to date its production to between 1450 and 1520.

It could be about:
▶ Alchemy
▶ Botany
▶ Astronomy
▶ Biology.

Its language has some European characteristics (but surprisingly few one- or two-letter words), or has been suggested as deriving from Hebrew,

Ukrainian or Manchurian. If its message is deliberately concealed, possibilities cited include:

▶ A cipher that fails to respond to any decryption technique.

▶ A set of code words.

▶ A stenographic system (say, every third letter).

▶ A grille.

It could, of course, be a hoax. The Voynich manuscript has been keeping its secrets at Yale University since 1969.

Pepys' diary

The famous diary of Samuel Pepys, English naval administrator and Member of Parliament, is often said to have been written in code, but this is not true. Pepys used Thomas Shelton's shorthand system for most of his entries (see illustration, below), with the more private information in a

Thomas Shelton's shorthand system was based on using symbols for letters of the alphabet.

mixture of languages including Latin, French and Spanish. By the time the diary was found and translation attempted, Shelton's symbols had been all but forgotten, and it was assumed that Pepys had written in cipher. Written during the 1660s, the diary is famous for Pepys' first-hand accounts of the coronation of King Charles II and the Great Fire of London.

Poe the code king

Perhaps more than any other writer, Edgar Allan Poe is identified with the subject of codes and ciphers. As a journalist, he challenged readers to create a cipher he could not break, and showed enormous skill in 'spinning' tales of his success in this. One of his most popular stories is *The Gold Bug*, which features invisible inks and a cryptogram solved by a frequency count. Its newspaper serialization and

A substitution cipher created by Edgar Allan Poe.

)	A	?	I/J	☞	R
(	B	!	K	]	S
—	C	&	L	[	T
✳	D	O	M	£	U/V
•	E	✎	N	$	W
,	F	†	O	¿	X
;	G	‡	P	¡	Y
:	H	¶	Q	☚	Z

subsequent publication in 1845 inspired great public interest in codes and ciphers, which was further stimulated by the launch of the telegraph system with its expensive 'pay by the word' charges (see page 34). Poe also wrote articles on ciphers in one of which he included the substitution cipher illustrated on the opposite page.

A master self-promoter, Poe was also a renowned hoaxer and a lover of mysteries. It has been suggested that he initiated one of the most famous tales in cryptographic history: the story of Thomas Beale.

The Golden ciphers

Thomas Beale was a mysterious figure who stayed for a while in 1820 at the Washington Hotel in Lynchburg, Virginia, disappeared for 18 months, and returned, entrusting a locked iron box to the hotel manager. He was never seen again, and it was not until 1845 that the manager, Robert Morriss, broke the container open. He found three sheets covered with numbers and a note from Beale explaining that the ciphers gave the location of a hidden trove of silver and gold that he had mined with 29 other men.

Unable to solve the ciphers, Morriss eventually asked a friend to put together a pamphlet telling the story and including the Beale papers. It was published in 1885 at a selling price of 50 cents. One of the ciphers was found to be a book code using the text of the American Declaration of Independence, broadly describing the spot where thousands of pounds in weight of silver and gold were buried.

Despite countless hours of analysis (some people seem to have spent a lifetime on it), no one has ever solved the two other ciphers, one of which supposedly gives the exact location of the treasure. It has been suggested that these, too, are book codes, based on a text written by Beale himself, which has since been lost, rendering the cipher unbreakable. Others speculate that they are a nomenclator (a mixture of cipher and code which, again without a key, makes then indecipherable). However, there are questions about:

▶ Whether Beale in fact ever existed at all.

▶ Why his 29 colleagues never made contact with Morriss to try to collect their share of the treasure.

▶ Why Beale would have used a public text for one cipher but not, apparently, for the others.

▶ Alleged similarities in writing style in the pamphlet and Beale's letter suggested they were from the pen of the same person.

▶ Whether the whole story is a hoax, possibly concocted by Edgar Allan Poe himself, or by the agent for the pamphlet, James B. Ward.

Elementary, my dear Watson

Sir Arthur Conan Doyle's famous fictional detective Sherlock Holmes applied his deductive powers (usually studying letter frequency) to several codes, including:

▶ A message concealed as every third word in *The 'Gloria Scott'*.

▶ A book code created by arch foe Moriarty using *Whitaker's Almanac* in *The Valley of Fear*.

▶ An unusual cipher using stick men symbols in *Adventure of the Dancing Men*. There are 26 of them, so each represents a letter of the alphabet (see the illustration above, which spells out 'Am here Abe Slaney').

Other books that feature codes include:

▶ Jules Verne's *Voyage to the Centre of the Earth* features a baffling code that turns out to be Latin written in reverse that can be read through the back of the paper.

▶ William Makepeace Thackeray included a Cardano grille (see pages 51–3) in his 1852 *The History of Henry Esmond*.

▶ H. Rider Haggard used a cipher in *Colonel Quaritch, QV*.

▶ Agatha Christie used a flower-names code in *The Four Suspects*, solved by the indomitable Miss Marple.

▶ Mystery writer Dorothy L. Sayers used a message in Playfair cipher (see pages 104–5) as a fundamental part of the plot in her 1932 Lord Peter Wimsey novel *Have His Carcass*. He solves it by guessing that the message starts with the name of a city and then a year, providing him with a crib.

The Shadow

The Shadow magazine published serialized stories for 18 years from 1931, and remains a cult publication. The tales of the mysterious sleuth, written by newspaperman and magician Walter B. Gibson

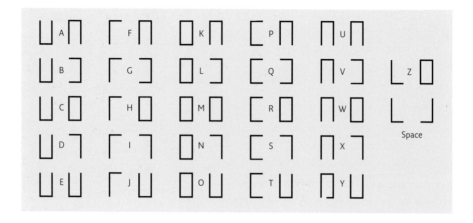

A simple substitution cipher broken by The Shadow – which is hardly surprising as it will fall to frequency analysis.

under the pen name Maxwell Grant, featured various codes in various ways. One, a simple set of substitution symbols (see illustration, above), is rather grandly referred to as 'one of the most unique methods of cryptic writing that had ever been devised', which is over-selling it somewhat. However, another cipher used in the same story, 'Chain of Death', features an inventive alphabet, and is illustrated below.

This cipher from one of the Shadow stories is far more interesting when combined with the instruction symbols on the next page.

So far this is just a graphically pleasing substitution alphabet, but the cipher was later refined with an additional four symbols:

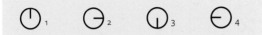

Each symbol indicates a degree of rotation, adding three levels of transposition to the alphabet. For example, a half turn shown by symbol 3 transforms the character for 'a' into that of B, and 'c' becomes D.

The Shadow was brought to life in a radio serial in the 1930s, a period when public interest in secret codes was high. Secret decoders were popular toys and promotional gifts from the 1930s onwards, especially from manufacturers of children's drinks and cereals. The *Captain Midnight* radio serial in the 1930s and 1940s included secret codes giving clues about the next episode and listeners could send in for a working cipher disc as part of a 'Spy-Detector Writer' kit, which could be used to decrypt messages broadcast in the show.

The Da Vinci Code

Dan Brown's 2003 bestseller *The Da Vinci Code* uses a number of ideas relating to cryptology and secret messages, such as:

▶ A message written with a black light pen begins 'PS', which is a code naming one of the people in the book and known only by that character.

▶ Three cryptic messages written in blood turn out to be a number code for a safe using the Fibonacci sequence (a series of numbers in which each is the

must know

Code play
Hugh Whitemore's 1986 play
Breaking the Code deals with the
life and death of Bletchley Park
code breaker Alan Turing. It was
adapted for television in 1995.

sum of the two previous numbers, so it begins 0, 1, 1, 2, 3, 5, 8, 13, 21), and two anagrams.

▶ There is a Bible reference, which turns out to be a red herring.

▶ The book features a 'cryptex', a word created by Brown to describe a cylindrical device invented by Leonardo Da Vinci for transporting secure messages, which can only be opened by turning letters to the correct sequence, clues to which are hidden in a riddle.

▶ Hidden symbolic messages in the shapes and colours of Leonardo Da Vinci's painting *The Last Supper*, and in the style and anagramatic title of his *Mona Lisa* portrait.

The Da Vinci Code has aroused huge controversy, partly because of its theme of religious manipulation, but also because some of the information presented as fact is inaccurate or merely hypothesis (for example, the *Mona Lisa* only received its popular title many years after Da Vinci's death). However, rather like Edgar Allan Poe in the 19th century, Brown has stirred interest in the field of cryptology and secret messages. There are, literally, millions of websites about the novel and its issues, and at least ten books.

Silver screen ciphers

Robert Harris' 1996 novel *Enigma* about the code-breaking heroics at Bletchley Park in World War II was made into a film in 2001. There are other films that feature codes:

▶ *Cryptonomicon* (1999) by Neal Stephenson, which features cryptography from World War II, including Enigma.

▶ Marlene Dietrich sends a message through the notes of the piano music she performs in the 1931 film *Dishonored*, a re-telling of the Mata Hari spy story from World War I.

▶ The James Bond book (1957) and film *From Russia with Love* (1963) features a decoding machine, that was christened Spektor in the book and then Lektor in the movie.

▶ The 1983 film *A Christmas Story* includes a re-telling of a myth that the *Little Orphan Annie* radio show broadcast a secret message that deciphered as 'Be sure to drink your Ovaltine', promoting the show's sponsor.

▶ The 2001 film *U-571* tells the fictional story of some American submariners getting an Enigma machine by hijacking a German submarine.

Book codes in the movies

Book and especially Bible codes are popular in Hollywood movies.

▶ In the 1996 film *Mission: Impossible* there are several references to Job 3:14: 'with kings and their advisors whose palaces lie in ruins'.

▶ The 2002 thriller *Red Dragon* features numerous apparent Bible citations, which turn out to refer to a different book, *The Joy of Cooking*. This may be less of a surprise when you consider the film is a sequel to the cannibalistic *Silence of the Lambs* (1991).

▶ *National Treasure* (2004) has a plot based around a code hidden in the US Constitution revealing the whereabouts of a treasure buried during the 1700s.

Art and music

It could be argued that all art is a code, as it is loaded with meanings that are not necessarilly immediately clear and require interpretation. These examples are of explicit use of codes.

The code of symbolism

Artists have used symbolism in their paintings for centuries, as a short cut to communicating ideas and connections. For example:

▶ Apples symbolize the fall of humankind (from the Garden of Eden).

▶ A lily represents purity.

▶ Lambs are a symbol of gentleness and innocence.

▶ Skulls represent mortality.

Mysterious monument

In the grounds of Shugborough Hall, a stately home in Staffordshire, is the so-called Shepherd's Monument, which bears some inscriptions that have baffled people for 250 years. Dating from the 1760s, the marble slab features the letters O, U, O, S, V, A, V and V with a D and an M below, etched under a mirror image of a painting by Nicholas Poussin. Some suggest the painting indicates the letters are supposed to be read in reverse. Solutions offered include:

▶ It is a set of instructions on how to find the Holy Grail.

▶ The markings are linked to the Masons and African nature worship.

▶ It is an ancient love note, and the code is a romantic Latin phrase.

Coded sculpture

Just outside the Central Intelligence Agency's (CIA's)
headquarters in Langley, Virginia is 'Kryptos', a 12-
foot-high copper, granite and petrified wood
sculpture that has baffled staff and other
cryptologists since its installation in 1990. Sculptor
James Sanborn, an ex-CIA worker, inscribed it with
some 1,800 letters forming four messages, each in a
different cipher.

Three of the ciphers have been broken using
frequency analysis and a Vigènere square. They
reveal a set of coordinates, possibly of a nearby
location where Sanborn has buried something. The
fourth passage has remained impenetrable.

Codes in music

Composer Edward Elgar loved puzzles and codes,
and managed to create a musical puzzle of his own
in his *Enigma Variations*, a series of musical
character portraits that is one of his best-loved
works. In all, 14 people and a dog are featured in the
variations: the people are identified by initials,
except for the 13th variation, which may have been
about a lover who had left England. Elgar also
revealed that he 'hid' a well-known tune into the
fabric of the score, and musical detectives are still
trying to find it.

Elgar's other cipher

Elgar was the author of the Dorabella cipher, a note sent to his friend Dora Penny in 1897. It comprises 87 squiggly characters at various angles in three neat lines. No one has managed to decipher it and it is thought it may have been linked to the mystery surrounding his *Enigma Variations*.

Do, re, mi, fa, sol, la, code

Composers have long been able to use letters identified with musical notation to build words into their music. There are two methods:
▶ The Sol Fa scale creates the syllables do, re, mi, fa, sol, la, and si/ti, represented by the notes C, D, E, F, G, A and B.
▶ Western notation uses the letters A to G but in German musical tradition B is also known as H, and E flat represents S, providing a somewhat limited but usable alphabet.

Baroque composers often used these letters to weave the names of friends or places into their music, and Johann Sebastian Bach was particularly fond of spelling out his surname. Robert

Schumann's *Piano Variations on the ABEGG Theme* records the name of a woman he was in love with: Meta Abegg.

Russian composer Dmitri Shostakovich frequently represented himself with the musical motif DSCH. He also used the sequence EAEDA to represent his student Elmira Nasirova, creating the 'word' E, La, Mi, Re, A.

Various musicians have namechecked modernist composer John Cage by spelling out his surname in their music, and his 1990 death is mourned in the *Penguin Café Orchestra*'s haunting track *CAGE DEAD*.

did you know?

Blocks rock
International rock band Coldplay used Emile Baudot's 1870 binary code to create the set of coloured blocks on the artwork of their 2005 release *X&Y*. The shapes are loose representations of the letters of the CD's title achieved by using binary code to decide whether to have a block or a gap. The colours are irrelevant.

A code chronology

Date	Event
C.1900 BC	Some Egyptian hieroglyphs are written in non-standard characters, a code apparently intended to add a little mystery. Possibly as little as 250 years later a small part of the Leiden, or Ipuwer papyrus (dates much disputed) was partly in cipher
C.1500 BC	A Sumerian pottery glaze recipe is written in code
500–600 BC	Hebrew scribes use the Atbash cipher
487 BC	Greek use of the scytale device is recorded
50–60 BC	Julius Caesar's shift cipher is used
AD 0–400 (date unknown)	The *Kama Sutra of Vatsayana* lists cryptography as the 44th and 45th of 64 arts (yogas) for men and women
805–873	Lifespan of Abu Al-Kindi, the first genuine cryptanalyst
C.1214–94	Lifespan of Roger Bacon (Dr Mirabilis), who described ciphers in use
1379	Gabrieli di Lavinde publishes the first-known nomenclators
1391	*Treatise on the Astrolabe*, attributed to English poet Geoffrey Chaucer, contains some enciphered passages
1412	*Subh al-a'sha*, a 14-volume encyclopedia written by Shihab al-Din al-Qalqashand, includes material on cryptology

1466-7	Leon Battista Alberti invents the cipher disc to allow encryption using two alphabets
16th century	Religious disputes make secret communication more important, stimulating the use of nomenclators and ciphers and the growth of the deciphering 'black chambers'
1516	First printed book on cryptology, *Steganographia* by Johannes Trithemius, is published
1563	Giovanni Battista Porta creates the first-known polygraphic substitution cipher
1586	Blaise de Vigenère publishes his Vigenère square
1587	Mary Stuart is executed after her codes are broken
17th century	Antione and Bonaventure Rossignol develop the Great Cipher (date of creation unknown)
1623	Francis Bacon produces his bilateral code
1781	Benjamin Franklin invents the homophonic substitution cipher
1790s	Thomas Jefferson invents his cipher cylinder, then forgets about it
1791	Optical telegraph is demonstrated
1811	Major George Scovell cracks the French codes, helping Wellington win the Peninsular War
1838	Morse code is invented
1844	Invention of the electric telegraph stimulates new interest in code making
1854	Playfair cipher is invented by Charles Wheatstone

A code chronology

1891	Bazieres cylinder a re-invention of the Jefferson wheel
1914-18	World War I encourages the development and use of ciphers and field codes and cryptanalysis
1914	Code-breaking Room 40 is set up at Admiralty House, London
1917	US enters the war as a result of the deciphered Zimmerman telegram
1918	Gilbert S. Vernam and Joseph Mauborgne devise the Vernam cipher one-time pad
1924	Enigma machine first shown
1939-45	Codes and ciphers play an important role in concealing and revealing communications during World War II
1974	Story of how Enigma had been solved is told
1976	Diffie-Hellman-Merkle key exchange scheme introduces the idea of public key encryption
1977	RSA algorithm makes public key encryption feasible
1990s	The rapid global rise of the internet and email communication highlights the issue of digital cryptography
1990	First research is published on quantum cryptography
1991	Phil Zimmerman releases his Pretty Good Privacy program

Code-breaking checklist

A variety of code-breaking methods are mentioned in this book where relevant to certain types of code or cipher. However, a summary of approaches can be useful.

Collect all the data
Gather all the encoded messages together. The more material you have at this stage, the more leads there are to follow.

Is it a simple code?
Study the text carefully to see if any of it makes sense. Look for the balance of vowels and consonants. Could it be an anagram? Check for embedded words or letters by looking at initial letters, and try counting every second, third or fourth (etc.) letter. Look at the start of the message and consider if any of it could contain instructions for the decoder: 1/5, for example, might indicate that the plaintext is contained in every fifth letter. There may also be clues if a keyword or date has been used (see 'Identifying the key' below).

Code suppositions
If it seems likely groups of characters each represent a word or phrase, remember they were put together in a dictionary, most probably in alphabetical order. So lower value numbers are likely to refer to words beginning with letters that appear earlier in the alphabet, and vice versa.

---

must know

The method
The scientific process for code breaking is:
► Analysis (letter counting, etc.)
► Hypothesis (guesswork)
► Prediction (if you find 'e', other letters become clearer)
► Verification (you were right!) or
► Refutation (start again, checking if what you think you know is correct)
This method takes you through three stages:
► Identification of the code type
► Breaking the code to see how it works
► Setting, which is the term for decrypting individual messages.

Word breaks

It is a major advantage if the ciphertext is still broken down into words, in which case it will be in groups varying in size between one and about eight characters, with the majority of words being three, four or five letters long. If the groups are larger but still irregular, each letter may be represented by more than one character as in a Baconian or binary code.

If word lengths are clear, look for one, two and three letter words. Check them against the list of the most common ones on page 84. Look for the definite or indefinite article ('the', 'a' or 'an') at the start of sentences.

In continuous ciphertext, the word (or, more often, sentence) breaks may be indicated by a null, the most obvious being an X or some other repeated character or pattern. Bear in mind that punctuation takes up nearly a fifth of typical text. Identifying the starts of sentences allows you to make more informed guesses about likely words, and therefore initial letters, at those points in the ciphertext.

Cribs and context

If part of the message is in plaintext (i.e. not encoded or enciphered), read up to the enciphered words and consider the context. Could they be names, places or numbers? If not, it is likely to be more technical language that is being concealed, so consider the overall context of the message: is it about battle preparations, finance, romance, etc.?

You may be able to find a crib. Does the message (or, far more usefully, do the *messages*) appear to start or finish in a formal way? Are any sections of two messages the same, in word length or character pattern? If you know something of the context, what words or phrases might you expect to find? Sometimes you can create your own crib. Assume that the message starts with the letter 'a'. Work out the key letter that could have encrypted 'a' into the first ciphertext letter. Try that key on the first letters of the other messages. Then repeat, assuming the first letter is 'b'. Each time, look for patterns in the lists of letters.

Letter frequency

Make a frequency chart for each character in the ciphertext. Refer to the letter frequency information on pages 82–5. The most common letter in English is 'e', which will appear noticeably more often than others in a monoalphabetic cipher. The frequency table will give you clues as to other common letters.

Once you can identify a common letter, you can make more informed guesses about its neighbours (for example a three-letter word ending in 'e' is very likely to be 'the'). You can also look for common letter patterns such as 'ing' (which is particularly useful as it ends a word, giving you less options to check for the start of the next word).

If the encryption is polyalphabetic, there will be no marked differences in character frequency, but there may still be discernible patterns. These can help you identify the key.

Identifying the key

If you suspect a key was used to encrypt, look for any indications from the sender of what the keyword is – it may not have been agreed in advance.

Encryption using a keyword can be attacked by guessing the length of the keyword. This can be achieved by exploiting the fact that certain patterns (such as 'th' or 'ed' are likely to appear very frequently in the plaintext and so may at some stages have been encoded with the same ciphertext letters. Number each character by position (1st, 2nd, 3rd, and so on). Now look for any repeated patterns (say, repeated pairs or triplets of letters or numbers).

Count how many characters there are between the start of each repeated pattern. If you find that certain pairs of characters appear after 54, then 120, then 96, then 186 ciphertext letters, you can turn to mathematics to help. Try dividing each of these numbers by three, then four, then five, and so on. Disregard any answers that are not whole. In this case, you will find that each number is divisible by both three and six. This suggests the keyword used to encipher was either three or six letters long. The lower figure seems unlikely, so try six first. Now you can test the assumption that the enciphering pattern is repeated every six letters by putting the ciphertext into six columns and carrying out frequency analysis on each column, because those letters are likely to have been enciphered with the same letter.

For example, if part of the ciphertext read JAQLZSOUFBLWPNIAFYHJBIWLVCEUFCHBVVXX, and you assume from analysis of the full text that the keyword length is six, arranging the letters of this section into six columns produces:

J	A	Q	L	Z	S
O	U	F	B	L	W
P	N	I	A	F	Y
H	J	B	I	W	L
V	C	E	U	F	C
H	B	V	V	X	X

Frequency analysis of the full ciphertext might then reveal that the letters in the first three columns were shifted 3, 9 and 16 places respectively on a Vigenère square, producing a plaintext of:

g	r	a	?	?	?
l	l	y	?	?	?
m	e	s	?	?	?
e	s	t	?	?	?
s	t	o	?	?	?
e	s	e	?	?	?

This would show that the first three letters of the keyword are CIP. A combination of continued frequency analysis and guesswork of the keyword would reveal it as CIPHER, with the full plaintext in columns now known to be:

g	r	a	d	u	a
l	l	y	t	h	e
m	e	s	s	a	g
e	s	t	a	r	t
s	t	o	m	a	k
e	s	e	n	s	e

and the plaintext can be written as gradually the message starts to make sense.

This example shows that sometimes you will be able to work out part of the keyword used and from this discover the whole keyword. For example, if you are pretty sure the keyword has the letters ENC___T_ON, you can guess the full keyword is ENCRYPTION.

must know

History of decryption
The history of decryption is as long as that of encryption and there is only space here to show the initial basic steps. More information can be found at: www.bbc.co.uk/dna/h2g2/alaba ster/A613135 and www.vector-site.net/ttcode_01.html There are also brief descriptions of some attack methods on modern computer codes on pages 148–51.

Glossary

algorithm: A set of mathematical instructions forming a step-by-step procedure to encrypt or decrypt information.

ASCII: American Standard Code for Information Interchange, used to represent text in computers.

asymmetric key system: A cryptological system where a different, 'one-way' key is needed for encrypting and decrypting.

authentication: The process of confirming identity.

bigram: Pair of letters, syllables or words, commonly used as the basis for statistical analysis of text.

binary code: Code system using only two characters or numbers, O and 1.

black chamber: General term for the cryptological offices set up by various governments since the 16th century where intercepted messages were studied for decryption.

block cipher: A cipher in which blocks of text are enciphered in groups, usually each of 64 bits.

brute force attack: A decryption strategy where every possibility is tried until a solution is found.

Caesar-shift cipher: Cipher in which a letter is replaced by another, a set number of places along in the alphabet.

cipher: A process in which individual letters are re-ordered or replaced to conceal the meaning of a text.

ciphertext: Enciphered text.

clear text: Another term for plaintext or *en clair*.

code: A system in which words or phrases are re-ordered or replaced for concealment. The word 'code' comes from the Latin for 'book', 'codex'.

code book: The crucial 'dictionary' giving words and phrases and the character(s) to be used to represent them. For larger scale codes, a reverse dictionary is required for decryption.

crib: A section of known plaintext, which can be used to break a code or cipher.

cryptanalysis: The art of breaking codes and ciphers.

cryptography: The art of devising codes and ciphers.

cryptology: The general term for cryptanalysis and cryptography.

cryptosystem: A system for encrypting and decrypting data.

decipher: Turn enciphered text into the original message, or plaintext.

decode: Turn a coded text into the original message, or plaintext.

decryption: The process of turning encoded or enciphered text into plaintext.

DES: The Data Encryption Standard, the algorithm widely used for data encryption, adopted in 1976.

Diffie-Hellman-Merkle key exchange: Process for establishing a secret key through public discussion.

digital signature: Electronic identification of a person, using a public key algorithm.

digraph: Two letters representing one sound, such as 'ph' or 'th', forming common pairings that are useful in decryption.

encode: Turn plaintext into a coded message.

encipher: Turn plaintext into a cipher message.

Enigma: Most famous enciphering system in recent history, used by the Germans in World War II and, crucially, broken by the British.

en clair: Plaintext, un-encoded message.

fractionation: Process in which plaintext symbols are converted into new symbols prior to transposition, creating a more complex cipher.

frequency analysis: Decryption strategy in which ciphertext letters are counted to identify patterns, which relate to how often letters occur in natural text.

Greek square: Device for changing characters into numbers, using the grid references of a square. Also known as the Polybius square or the Greek checkerboard.

homophonic substitution: A cipher where a letter can be represented by several different characters, thus combating frequency analysis.

key: The set of characters that determines how a text is to be encrypted.

key length: The number of characters or bits in the key. The longer it is, the harder it is to decrypt.

monoalphabetic substitution cipher: Cipher in which the plaintext is encrypted using one alphabet.

nomenclator: Encryption using a mixture of homophonic substitution and codes for certain words and phrases. It was the main cryptological method for several centuries until World War I.

null: Part of the ciphertext, which indicates ends of sentences, or which can be ignored in decryption because it is there to confuse enemy code breakers.

one-time pad: The only known totally secure encryption method – a running key of totally random characters, used only once.

plaintext: The message before it is encrypted and after it is decrypted.

Polybius checkerboard: *see* Greek square.

polyalphabetic cipher: Cipher in which the plaintext is encrypted using more than one alphabet.

Pretty Good Privacy (PGP): A method for secure encrypted email communication developed by Phil Zimmerman.

private key: The 'secret' part of an asymmetric key system, also known as the decryption key.

public key: The 'open' part of an asymmetric key system, also known as the encryption key.

quantum cryptography: The use of quantum physics to create random bits on a computer, which can be used to create a one-time pad cipher.

running key: A key as long as the plaintext, as in a book cipher.

RSA: Rivest, Shamir and Adleman's system enabling public key cryptography, invented in 1977.

steganography: Greek for 'hidden writing', this is the art of hiding the message itself, rather than concealing its meaning.

substitution cipher: Encryption system in which letters are replaced but remain in the correct position.

superencryption: Encrypting a message twice, either with the same or with a different method for the second process. Also known as superencipherment.

tabula recta: A square table of alphabets, each shifted one place to the left.

Transposition cipher: Encryption system in which letters change position, creating a giant anagram (in which the letters are also changed).

Vigenère cipher: The first polyalphabetic cipher made using a tabula recta combined with a keyword.

Books

Applied Cryptography, Bruce Schneier (Wiley Publishing, 1995) and
Secrets and Lies, Bruce Schneier (Wiley Publishing, 2004) deal with the practice and issues of
    computerized cryptography
Codes and Ciphers, Robert Churchhouse (CUP, 2002) gives a good briefing with many examples
Codes, Ciphers and Secret Writing, Martin Gardner (Dover Publications, 2002) is good on simple
    codes
Cryptography: A Very Short Introduction, Fred Piper and Sean Murphy (OUP, 2002) is a good briefing
    on modern trends
Cryptography: The Science of Secret Writing, Laurence Dwight Smith (Dover Publications, 1971)
    covers simple codes

General histories
The Code Book, Simon Singh (Fourth Estate, 1999) covers the story of codes
The Codebreakers, David Khan (Scribner, 1996) is the classic work on the history of codes

Specific histories
The Man Who Broke Napoleon's Codes, Mark Urban (Faber and Faber, 2001) is the story of William
    Scovell
Navajo Weapon: The Navajo Code Talkers, Sally McClain (Rio Nuevo, 2002)
Navajo Code Talkers, Andrew Santella (Compass Point Books, 2004)
The Victorian Internet, Tom Standage (Weidenfeld and Nicolson, 1998) tells the story of the
    telegraph system

Websites

The history of codes
http://fly.hiwaay.net/~paul/cryptology/history.html covers the early history of cryptography
www.axsmith.net/encryption.htm
www.bbc.co.uk/history/ancient/egyptians/decipherment_03.shtml
www.brooklynmuseum.org/exhibitions/2003/egypt-reborn/ancient-
    egypt/k4/language/language05
www.freemaninstitute.com/Gallery/rosetta.htm
hem.passagen.se/tan01/simsub.html has examples of simple substitutions
www.jproc.ca/crypto/crypto_hist.html has a timeline of cryptography
www.murky.org/archives/cryptography/ has lots on history and development
www.simonsingh.com/ website of the author of the excellent *The Code Book*
www.thebritishmuseum.ac.uk/compass/ixbin/goto?id=OBJ67home.ecn.ab.ca/~jsavard/crypto/
    entry.htm

www.vectorsite.net/idsearch.html tells the story of codes with plenty on their American history and on breaking codes

www.world.std.com/~cme/html/timeline.html has a chronology of cryptography

Sites for children and beginners:

http://search.looksmart.com/p/browse/us1/us317837/us317922/us903634/us10124254/ has links to sites for children

www.google.com/intl/xx-piglatin/ translates messages into Pig Latin

www.scouting.org.za/codes/

www.10ticks.co.uk/s_codebreaker.asp allows you to email coded messages to your friends

Sites with specialist information

ftp://ftp.pgpi.org/pub/pgp/6.5/docs/english/IntroToCrypto.pdf comprehensive site on all aspects of modern cryptography

http://members.tripod.com/~mr_sedivy/colorado44.html has examples of the cowboy branding alphabet

http://64.233.183.104/search?q=cache:1NJETIbMh7gJ:www.cs.arizona.edu/icon/analyst/backiss /IA62.pdf+%22battista+Porta%22+digraphic+cipher&hl=en for a version of the Porta digraphic cipher

http://starbase.trincoll.edu/~crypto/historical/railfence.html for rail fence and scytale ciphers

www.aldertons.com/index.htm cockney rhyming slang dictionary

www.cia.gov/cia/information/tour/krypt.html CIA website on kryptos

www.codesandciphers.org.uk/documents/ includes the 1944 Bletchley Park cryptographic dictionary

www.cockneyrhymingslang.co.uk/cockney/ cockney rhyming slang dictionary

www.comsoc.org/livepubs/ci1/public/anniv/pdfs/hellman.pdf article giving an overview on modern public cryptography

www.cs.dartmouth.edu/~jford/crypto.html gives background on quantum cryptography

www.fas.org/irp/world/uk/gchq/index.html unofficial website about GCHQ

www.gchq.gov.uk/ website of the UK signals intelligence headquarters

www.elonka.com/kryptos site about the kryptos sculpture

www.geocities.com/Vienna/4056/cipher.html shows the Elgar code

www.history.navy.mil/faqs/faq61-2.htm contains information on Navajo code talkers

www.infosyssec.org/infosyssec/cry1.htm has lots of background and current information on security

www.nationalarchives.gov.uk/spies/ciphers/default.htm

www.pbs.org/wgbh/nova/decoding/ describes how the Nazi party coded their messages for privacy

www.pepysdiary.com/archive/1660/04/25/index.php website about Pepys' diary

www.profactor.at/~wstoec/rsa.html has a step-by step-guide to public encryption

www.schneier.com/crypto-gram.html monthly newsletters on computer cryptography for industry

www.voynich.nu/ on Voynich manuscript

Miscellaneous other sites

http://elonka.com/UnsolvedCodes.html

http://eprint.iacr.org/ an archive of papers on cryptology

http://mad.home.cern.ch/frode/crypto/ lists many papers on post-war codes

www.faqs.org/faqs/cryptography-faq/part01/index.html answers your questions on cryptography

www.gchq.gov.uk/codebreaking/ is the site of the British government's communications experts, and has puzzles and games

www.nsa.gov/history/index.cfm website of the USA National Security Agency

www.nsa.gov/museum/index.cfm website of the national cryptologic museum in the US

www.puzz.com/cryptoquotes.html has cryptograms of sayings by famous people

www.spymuseum.org/index.asp website of the international spy museum in the US

www.und.nodak.edu/org/crypto/crypto/.sample-issue.html is the website of the American cryptogram association, which was set up in the 1920s.

Sites about the Beale papers

http://bealeciphers.tripod.com/ discusses the Beale story

http://66.249.93.104/search?q=cache:DZFvd__9EP4J:www.bealepapers.com/The%2520Last%2520Haunting%2520Publish.pdf+Thomas+Beale+Edgar+allan+poe&hl=en a website about the Beale papers

http://smd173.tripod.com/Beale/BealePapers.htm has the full text of the Beale papers

http://unmuseum.org/beal.htm deals with the Beale story.

Computer short cuts and symbols

en.wikipedia.org/wiki/Leet has an alphabet of leet symbols

http://tronweb.super-nova.co.jp/characcodehist.html has a brief history of ASCII character codes

www.acronymfinder.com/ gives definitions for acronyms and abbreviations

www.lingo2word.com/lists/txtmsg_listA.html txt lingo

www.microsoft.com/athome/security/children/kidtalk.mspx? A parents' guide to computer slang

www.smsglossary.com/what-is-sms.html

www.techdictionary.com/emoticons.html dictionary of text short cuts with symbols

www.t-mobile.com/mytmobile/communication/messaging/shorthand.asp about text short cuts

Index

Index

Acknowledgments

Thanks to Ivy Jones and Jonathon Parker for background information.

⚙ **Collins** need to know?

Look out for these recent titles in Collins' practical and accessible need to know? series.

Other titles in the series: